# Royalty
# Revealed

# Royalty Revealed

Unity Hall and Ingrid Seward

St. Martin's Press
New York

*For Derek, Olivia and Sue*

ISBN 0-312-03924-7

First published in Great Britain by Sidgwick & Jackson Limited.

First U.S. Edition
10  9  8  7  6  5  4  3  2  1

# Contents

Chapter 1   A Cast Of Characters      1

Chapter 2   Magic Childhood      24

Chapter 3   Upstairs Downstairs And Somewhere In Between      41

Chapter 4   Bobo      60

Chapter 5   On Stage At The Royal Court      68

Chapter 6   Money Matters      86

Chapter 7   At Their Majesties' Pleasure      102

Chapter 8   Travelling Royally      119

Chapter 9   Dressing The Part      134

Chapter 10   Escape      145

Chapter 11   The Head That Wears The Crown      158

    *Bibliography*      163

    *Index*      165

# A Cast Of Characters

The British Royal Family must be, of necessity, the most close-knit clan in the world. This highly privileged group, the House of Windsor, constantly renews itself by marriage but once someone from outside marries into this extraordinary family they slowly become engulfed. The relentless tentacles of the Monarchy close around until the newcomer is sucked into Royal life and made a true member of the family, all personal freedom gone.

But there are compensations – notably a life of unique luxury enriched by many, many perks which the family do not exactly advertise.

It is natural that newer recruits fresh from the outside world, such as the Princess of Wales, the Duchess of York and Princess Michael of Kent, at first fight to retain their individuality and cling to their own life-style and friends. But in time they come to realise and accept that friendships, as lesser mortals know them, can, sadly, for them no longer exist. Inevitably this unique group – and a curious collection they are when analysed – are forced into each other's company. In a precise and unchanging royal routine, the family and a few close and trusted friends crowd together for protection against the prying outside world. They congregate in the great Royal houses such as Balmoral and Sandringham where the broad surrounding acres allow some shelter and privacy.

Royalty form family circles. The inner circle consists of those closest to the Queen – her children, their children, her husband and her mother. Since they are the ones who have the most

1

difficulty in achieving any kind of private life they are especially welcome at every family gathering. The second circle contains lesser Royals who are invited into the inner circle if popular (like Princess Alexandra) or sometimes left out if not popular (like Princess Michael of Kent). Finally, there are the more distant cousins who are furthest from the special inner ring. Like any family, they are all quite different personalities and are not always intimate. Sometimes they are not even good friends.

As undisputed head of the clan, the Queen is the strongest of all and the quiet hub-star around which the entire family ultimately revolves. Her seal of approval is vital for each individual, especially for those marrying into the family. Fergie has always had it, so has the Princess of Wales, but Princess Michael's rebellious and sometimes unroyal behaviour did not go unnoticed. But she has recently redeemed herself by keeping an especially low profile. The flamboyant Princess even managed to resist fighting back when the media accused her of being out of favour because the Queen supposedly failed to invite her and her husband for Christmas at Sandringham.

The truth of the matter, it transpired, was that only the immediate family were present anyway, since Sandringham is small by Royal standards, and their normal Christmas meeting place, the spacious Windsor Castle, was undergoing renovations. The Duke and Duchess of Gloucester were at their country home, Barnwell Manor, in Northamptonshire; the Duke and Duchess of Kent were at theirs, Amner Hall on the Sandringham Estate, although they have since bought a small house in Nettlebed, Oxfordshire; and Prince and Princess Michael were at Nether Lypiatt in Gloucestershire. 'It was,' Princess Michael later confided, 'the first Christmas we had spent in our own home since we were married and I loved it.'

It is, however, unwise to fall foul of the Queen. She is totally confident in her role as Monarch and knows exactly what is expected of her and of her relatives. She also hopes, if not demands, that her family do what is required of them. Fortunately for the nation she is a traditionalist and has exactly the right temperament for the position she holds.

Little seems to change in Royal life, mostly because the Queen herself is such an immaculate creature of habit. She is totally predictable. Her staff say they can set their watches by her, from the time when, after her morning bath, she sits down to a hearty breakfast in her private dining room, right through to when her maid draws her second bath of the day before bed. Like millions of the lesser mortals she rules, the Queen finds that an evening bath is relaxing and helps her sleep.

Her Majesty has an iron will which reveals itself even in small ways. A lifetime's clothes, all carefully stored in Buckingham Palace, would still fit if she wished to wear them. Her weight and shape have hardly changed over the years. This is something of a tribute to that iron will – since her biggest problem is controlling her sweet tooth. Since the days when she was a child her favourite things have included sugared almonds, crêpe Suzette and the habit of dropping a little coffee sugar into her coffee, letting it half dissolve and eating it off the spoon. (She also treats her corgis to nibbles of the same sugar.)

Considering how much entertaining she has to do, it is quite remarkable that her weight has remained so constant, particularly as she does not bother with any kind of exercise routine. There are no exercise bicycles at the Palace, though her new daughter-in-law, the Duchess of York, exercises vigorously and Diana swims first thing most days in the Palace pool. The Queen believes that walking her dogs and riding – which she does every morning at 10.30 for an hour when she is out of London – are quite sufficient to keep her figure trim.

Her tastes are simple and those who know her well say that she is two different people – Lilibet (her pet name) and Her Majesty the Queen. Lilibet would much rather wear an inexpensive headscarf than a priceless tiara and would rather sit on the grass for a country picnic with her family, even in a chilling, showery wind, than attend some sumptuous, glittering State banquet. Less hardy folk have been known to complain that she is apparently quite impervious to cold.

Sometimes Lilibet and Her Majesty become one. In spite of her liking for casual clothes, the Queen always travels with her favourite jewellery, even on holiday. The priceless collection is carried in a special large brown leather suitcase, and has its own protective canvas cover across which, in black, are boldly printed the words THE QUEEN. Its safekeeping is the unsettling responsibility of her footman.

In the suitcase are seven sets of jewellery consisting of matching necklace, ear-rings and bracelet. The Queen wears these in rotation, a different set every day of the week. For a later holiday or visit, a different seven sets are chosen. The tweedy day-time lady of the grouse moors who walks behind the guns picking up the dead birds with dogs she has trained herself, becomes, during the evening, a regal glamorous figure at her own dinner table.

When asked to draw a picture of the Queen, children invariably portray her wearing a crown and crinoline dress. There are times in the middle of the day when the Queen looks exactly like this child's eye-view of her. Sometimes in the afternoon, usually at 3.30, she can be seen walking along the Buckingham Palace corridors wearing a magnificent ball gown, sparkling with jewels and crowned with a dazzling tiara. Her ubiquitous dogs are still with her, scampering around her feet. She is on her way to the Yellow Drawing Room which is used by those portrait artists fortunate enough to be commissioned to paint members of the family. This particular room is chosen because the light is good. Sometimes there will be two or three portraits of different members of the family on the go, the unfinished canvasses waiting for the next sitting.

Unless she is ill, the Queen goes to church on Sunday mornings in her role as 'Defender of the Faith'. She never misses this, not even when she is on board the Royal Yacht. Britannia's dining room doubles as a place of worship, holding a congregation of sixty – just the number of dining chairs this splendid ship carries. The Admiral who is in charge of the yacht takes the service and, as a rule, Prince Philip reads the lesson. The Queen dresses formally for the service, wearing a coat (one relegated to private duty) but not a hat. The gentlemen wear suits or their officers' uniforms.

In spite of a reluctance to interfere, the Queen will on rare occasions lay down the law when a member of the Royal group behaves in such a manner that could embarrass the whole pack of court cards. The Royal Family are not supposed to have personal problems, but in the Autumn of 1987 it was impossible for the public not to be aware that Prince Charles and Princess Diana were struggling through a serious marital crisis. They were rarely together and when they were seen in public they barely acknowledged each other. Hostility steamed between them. It wasn't necessary to be a psychologist to see that they had had some kind of blazing row, and that, stubbornly, neither was giving in.

'What makes it difficult for them,' Diana's father, the Earl of Spencer, explained, 'is that they are on show the whole time. They might have had a disagreement, but then they have to step out in front of the cameras and pretend that everything is going well, and that is not easy, as any couple would know.'

That summer Charles and Diana had plenty to row about. Diana, showing her independence, had spent hours dancing with a handsome young banker, Philip Dunne, at a society ball while Charles, who has never been a night owl, went home. Because Diana was dancing with such abandon, people talked, and it looked remarkably as if she had a crush on Dunne. Prince Charles meanwhile spent weeks without his family at Balmoral and was seen in the company of pre-marriage women friends like Lady Tyron and Camilla Parker Bowles. Both are happily married ladies, but this did not stop Diana being wildly jealous of them in the early days. Now she did not seem to care.

Once she most certainly did.

In the early days of their marriage, the fox hunt came through the Highgrove Garden just as Charles and Diana were about to have lunch, and the Prince rushed out to speak to Camilla Parker Bowles. And they talked and they talked and they talked! The Princess was not amused. She complained bitterly that lunch was spoiling, but that wasn't by any means the true reason for her irritation.

Her jealousy of Lady Tryon – Dale Tryon, the Australian nick-named 'Kanga' – was extreme. The Tryons had both been intimate friends of Charles for many years. Considering how close Charles and the Tryons had been (to the extent, for example, of sharing a private fishing holiday each year in a remote spot in Iceland), it did seem extraordinary that neither was invited to the wedding. Had Diana put her pretty foot down and decreed they would not be welcome?

Now, seven years later, this marital rift looked serious and the Queen felt she ought to intervene. The world-wide Press speculation, talk of separation or, worse, even divorce was becoming both dangerous and damaging. She summoned her son and daughter-in-law to her private sitting room at Buckingham Palace and told them that whatever was going on, it had to stop. And it was Charles who caught the rough edge of her tongue, presumably since she felt that he ought to know better. No-one except the two principal protagonists and possibly Prince Philip will ever know exactly what the Queen said. But whatever it was, her words were certainly effective. Slowly Charles and Diana came back to some sort of rapport. And in February of 1989 the Princess, looking stunning in a jade green jacket and matching wide-brimmed hat over a short black skirt, arrived at Philip Dunne's wedding in Kensington. He was marrying Domenica Fraser, daughter of a former Rolls Royce chairman. Significantly, Prince Charles stayed away, preferring to hunt in Wiltshire.

Today, it is simply not possible for the Royal Family to avoid those who watch them and it was the patience of a dogged photographer which caused the Queen to intervene in her son's family quarrel. Princess Diana had gone without the Prince to a dinner party at the Queensgate Mews, home of the heiress, Kate

Menzies. About midnight she emerged from the house in red trousers tucked into boots below a satin bomber jacket. Major David Waterhouse, another guest and a friend of the Princess, was already in his car. The Princess was dancing about in front of it, illuminated by the headlights and squealing as the car lurched towards her and he pretended to run her down. Jason Fraser, the patient photographer, leapt from where he had been hiding and snatched a picture. Immediately Diana's detective, Ken Wharf, grabbed him, demanding the film. Jason refused to hand it over and an almighty row ensued. Finally, Diana herself came forward with tears in her eyes to beg for the film. To his astonishment, she told the photographer (who happens to be an attractive young man of about her own age) how miserable her life was, how few friends and little fun she had, and how if the picture were published, it would make things worse for her. She took a little block of white paper cards from her handbag and asked him to please to give her the film, write his name and address down for her, and then the rest of his pictures would be returned to him.

'I handed the film over to her,' said Jason. 'I wouldn't have done it for the detective. He was swearing at me all the way through. I met him the next morning in a coffee shop and by then he'd calmed down and couldn't have been pleasanter. He handed me back the developed pictures from the reel, minus the one of Diana.'

The Palace do not like finding themselves in such a position, and therefore strive to thwart the royal watchers. And in turn, the inquisitive watchers strive to feed a public constantly hungry for the tiniest tit-bit of inside information.

The Windsors have learned the hard way that it is not possible to confide or chatter indiscreetly to anyone – except perhaps another member of the family.

But secrets do get out. And royal scandals do occur. It is then, when the Press pounces and the cameras zoom, that the family are at their strongest, closing royal ranks. Giving nothing away. Publicly, they rarely explain, rarely complain. Doggedly they present a bland, united, silent front. They do not confirm, neither do they deny. They behave as if absolutely nothing, simply nothing, had happened.

Even within the family group, disasters are seldom mentioned. Princess Margaret's sometimes odd lifestyle is ignored. So are Angus Ogilvy's problems, the Duchess of Kent's intense behaviour and Fergie's occasional lack of dignity. The Queen once called a meeting of Fleet Street editors to chastise them for their treatment of Lady Diana, but more usually, matters such as these are not mentioned inside, let alone outside, the tight magic Royal circle.

But certain indiscretions will make the Queen act. When her youngest son, Edward, quit the Royal Marines after only four months' service, Prince Philip was known to be furious. He is Honorary Captain General of the Regiment and, to his way of thinking, to quit is a crime. The family feelings became public when a letter to Commandant-General Sir Michael Wilkin, head of the Marines, expressing Philip's dismay was leaked to the *Sun* newspaper. Ignoring copyright laws, the Editor printed it. The Queen was very angry indeed. It cost the *Sun* an apology and a small fortune to a charity of Prince Philip's choice.

In the normal run of events, the Queen rarely gets really angry or lets her feelings show. Shouting at people is most certainly not her style. She leaves that to her husband. He is inclined to shout rather a lot – either at his staff or, frequently, at Prince Charles. Charles, slower and more thoughtful than his father, irritates Prince Philip, particularly when they are out shooting together. A nature lover, Charles is often distracted when they are out on the moors. If he spots something that interests him in the surroundings he will linger and look. This has been known to cause a bad-tempered Prince Philip to bawl at his son: 'Move your bloody arse!'.

Those who work at the Palace cannot recall ever hearing the Queen raise her voice in anger. Anything that she feels is disrespectful to the Monarchy, however, does make her angry. There was such an occasion when President and Mrs Reagan visited Britain in 1982 as the Queen's guests at Windsor Castle. The President said that he would like to ride with the Queen in Windsor Great Park. She duly organised this and agreed for the media to be present.

The reporters and cameramen who were recording the event then began shouting questions at the President. He, with great good humour and a touch of banter, answered in just the same way as he would have done in the more informal USA.

Now, the Queen might just be heard to say a good morning to a reporter (and only then if he's lucky) but jokey conversations with the media are definitely out, and in this instance she felt that the President was turning this encounter into an informal press reception and using her for political purposes. She was furious, so she wheeled her horse around and rode away.

But the Queen is, first and foremost, a diplomat. Aware that the President must have noticed her fury (since everyone else had) she found an opportunity at dinner that night to smooth over the situation. Casually she mentioned that her horse had been restless and she had thought it best to let him ride on.

She is seldom angry with her own family and her confrontation with Charles was a rare event. They are very, very close indeed and there is great loving warmth between them. The Queen never had time to be the perfect mother – her attitude to motherhood was not unlike that of her daughter, Anne, who said that 'being pregnant was an awfully boring time for one'. Something with which Princess Diana would heartily agree. While pregnant, she was frequently heard to mutter that if men had the babies there wouldn't be many of them about. The Princess Royal also admitted on television that she wasn't that crazy about children, with which Princess Diana most certainly would not agree. The Queen would not be so frank on the subject, but certainly in her youth, her husband always came first. If there were a possibility of being with Philip and that possibility meant that Anne and Charles had to be left at the Palace – at the Palace they were left. And later, once she became the Monarch, it was simply not possible to be a doting mother who was always there for the children. The demands on her time were great and her duty as the Queen had to come first.

When they were small, Prince Charles and Princess Anne probably saw as much of their grandmother as they did of their mother. Prince Charles reveres her, but then she is cherished and respected by everyone – her own family, her staff and the great majority of the nation itself.

The Queen made public her deep attachment to her mother when, in a surprising break with protocol, she gave the Queen Mother precedence at her eightieth birthday celebrations nine years ago. Queen Elizabeth the Queen Mother, as she is offically known, walked into St Paul's Cathedral after her daughter but out again ahead of her daughter. A reversal of the normal situation. And it was on the steps of St Paul's after that birthday thanksgiving service that the Queen Mother revealed she still has at least one ambition left. She would like to receive a congratulatory telegram from her daughter, the Queen, on her 100th birthday.

She was standing by the Queen's side as they both paused to wave to the happy crowds who had gathered to congratulate her. 'I have enjoyed it all so much,' she said misty-eyed. 'Now I really feel as if I can go on to be 100.'

The Queen pulled a wry face and whispered: 'In that case, you'll be getting the telegram from Charles. I doubt if I'll be around.'

Today the job of preserving the Monarchy may come first with the Queen, but preserving her family is a close second. She has deeply protective feelings towards her sister, Princess Margaret, even though when they were younger the temperamental Margaret showed unattractive flashes of jealousy towards her big sister.

The Queen and the King did spoil their younger daughter outrageously. She was such a pretty girl, and perhaps her parents were aware of her not always well-concealed envy of her sister. Her father in particular doted on her. If she were in the same room he could not take his eyes off her, and would compliment her publicly all the time. If she gave him a warm affectionate hug, his face would light up with pleasure.

'I know I shouldn't spoil her, but I can't help it . . .' he would say apologetically.

Eileen Parker, ex-wife of Commander Mike Parker who was Prince Philip's Private Secretary in the first years of the Queen's reign, was aware that the younger Princess irritated Prince Philip. It seemed he thought her vain and frivolous. Eileen Parker recalls how Philip once saw a harassed footman rushing down the Buckingham Palace corridors carefully holding a hatbox.

'What's the hurry?' he asked.

'It's Princess Margaret's tiara,' the footman explained. 'She's waiting for it.'

Prince Philip responded sarcastically.

'Of course,' he said. 'It's the first time she's ever worn one in public and she's *very* excited about it.'

Once, not long after he had become engaged to the young Princess Elizabeth, a friend jokingly asked why he hadn't picked the pretty one. Philip was furious. 'You wouldn't say that,' he replied angrily, 'if you knew her.'

The pretty one has had the saddest life. As the second daughter of George VI, Margaret was designated Regent in the event of the premature death of the Queen when Prince Charles was too young to accede. In 1953 Princess Margaret was ousted and replaced on the Regency Council by Prince Philip. She must have felt that he had taken everything away from her – the companionship of her sister, now her position and, indeed, it was he who insisted that marriage to her divorced boyfriend, Peter Townsend, was impossible. Margaret and Philip had never particularly liked each other. Prince Philip was always in her way. He made his disapproval of her obvious and plagued her with his cold sardonic teasing. And ever since her historic renouncement of Peter Townsend, she and Prince Philip have had little to say to each other.

Prince Philip may upset others, but there is no doubt that the

Royal marriage is a good one. This is primarily through the Queen's efforts. All their married life she has given Philip enough rope for him to follow all the way home, and she firmly believes that at home, the man must be the head of the family. Prince Philip may walk two paces behind her in public but within the privacy of their Palaces, and for anything to do with family matters, he is very much the boss. But, of course, in the wider scheme of things he is not. There is a Palace story (undoubtedly apocryphal) that on hearing God Save the Queen being played, Elizabeth joked, 'They're playing my tune.'

A true story is that Princess Margaret used to tease her father, King George VI, asking him, 'Papa, do you sing God Save Thy Gracious Me?'.

Another true story tells of the Queen and Philip dining together at the Embassy in Paris in the early 1970s before going to a reception. (The Queen favours receptions as it prevents being stuck with the same people for the two-hour length of a dinner.) Outside a military band began to play. Prince Philip cocked an ear: 'That's my Regiment,' he said.

'No, it is not,' said the Queen firmly. 'It is mine.' And of course it was. They all are.

Sometimes for a man of great ability and energy as Philip is, this must be galling. Perhaps it is always being two paces behind that has made him more arrogantly royal in his attitudes than any of his family. And he has always found the cage of Royal life restricting.

The trouble with Philip is that while he enjoys the privileges of Royalty, he bitterly resents the public and media interest in his family. He seems never to have accepted that everything has a price – including living in Palaces.

He has always battled to keep his life as private as possible and finds intrusion infuriating, particularly at Balmoral where the family's 50,000 acres cannot be entirely protected from either picnickers or pressmen. He tried littering the estate with 'No Trespassing' and 'Private Property' notices. Neither worked. Cameramen still lurked and the public still walked over the land. Then the Prince had a brainwave. New notices were posted.

They warned 'Beware of Adders'. Highly effective they were too.

There are those of the Royal Family who are pretty wary of him. He has his champions – he and Princess Alexandra have always been the best of friends – but if Princess Margaret is not his greatest fan, neither is the Queen Mother. They also have little to say to each other. He is never in London for her birthday – it clashes with Cowes Week which he never misses. They have a drink in the same company on Sunday morning after church, and that's about it. But then he and the Queen Mother have so little in common. She is cosy; he abrasive. She is not an intellectual but very much a sybarite whereas he likes an out-door life and talking to brilliant people. Fortunately, the Queen is a highly intelligent woman – she could hardly be anything else since she has entertained and been entertained by some of the best brains in the world.

Prince Charles is also wary of his father. They are not in the least alike, even in small ways. Charles likes to relax in a bath. His father likes a fast, invigorating shower. Charles is the slowest eater in the family, with little appetite. His father, who has an enormous appetite, shoves food into his mouth to get it down as fast as possible. Prince Charles' water-colours are traditional, his father paints in a more modern style. Charles is fascinated by philosophy. Philip thinks it is a load of codswallop. Nevertheless, Charles has great respect for his father and admits that 'Papa is very wise'. And Philip does accept that 'Charles has his mother's serenity and concern for individuals'.

Charles and his mother have always been close. Until his marriage he relied on her greatly. She was always there for advice, even for simple problems such as which fabric to choose for a new suit.

When he neared thirty, she suggested that perhaps it was now time for him to see the private Cabinet papers. The Queen felt it was a necessary part of his training for eventual kingship, and he works as diligently at these papers as she herself does. Neither of them really needs to do it. The Queen could just scribble her signature on the endless documents and that would be the end of it. But she, and her son, are both interested and fascinated to know what is going on in Government.

But of course the Prince is painstaking and diligent with everything he undertakes. Leaving aside the Queen Mother, our future King is undoubtedly that simple thing, the *nicest* member of the Royal Family.

He was much influenced by his great uncle, the late Earl Mountbatten of Burma, whom he called his Honorary Grandfather. When Lord Mountbatten was assassinated in 1979, blown up by the IRA, Prince Charles was shattered. It was to Lord Mountbatten that the young Charles had always turned when he had a problem and to whom he confided how much he hated being in the Royal Navy. At first the Prince was bitterly unhappy when, of necessity, he went into the Navy. All Royal men must do their stint in the Queen's Armed Services. It was the loss of his privacy that he found hardest to bear. School had been difficult for the heir to the throne, but now he was thrown into a closer community than he had ever known before and he was finding it difficult to cope.

While Charles was stationed at HMS Vernon on the Isle of Wight he would flee to Broadlands, Lord Mountbatten's home in Hampshire, whenever he had a chance. One of the eight main rooms in the house was kept especially for him. His detective would drive him from the coast and he would dine alone with Lord Mountbatten who had been First Sea Lord. They talked over naval life and Mountbatten attempted to encourage the Prince from his own experience. After dinner the Prince would go to his room to read.

It was a lonely life for a young man, but when he was eventually made commanding officer of the minesweeper Bronnington, this seemed to be a turning point. He became more self-assured and it seemed to those near him that he suddenly grew up.

John Barratt, who was private secretary to Lord Mountbatten for more than twenty years, was aware of the special closeness between the young Prince and the aging sea-dog. He says the Prince has many of his great uncle's qualities. Devotion to duty, loyalty, an insatiable appetite for getting to know about things – and a reluctance to face the more unpleasant facts of life.

John Barratt tells a charming story which perfectly illustrates the quaint face of Royalty. He was living with his wife and two young daughters at Broadlands in one of the mews houses over the stables. The Queen, Prince Charles and Prince Philip were often in evidence, and though the children were not blasé about these encounters they were not particularly impressed, either.

Barratt's five-year-old girl, Mandy, was besotted by Lord Mount-batten's dog Juno. One day she spotted the dog in the stable yard and rushed downstairs. After a while her parents heard Mountbatten's voice talking to her and then another voice – it was Prince Charles.

They peered out of the window to make sure that Mandy wasn't making a nuisance of herself and were surprised to see Prince Charles bobbing up and down in the most extraordinary way while the little girl watched him gravely. When she returned upstairs, Mandy explained: 'I bumped into Prince Charles. Lord Mountbatten said I must curtsey to him, but I didn't know how. Prince Charles was teaching me.'

Mandy was always attempting to get a look at the Queen but it was an unspoken rule that if Her Majesty were riding at Broadlands everyone kept out of the way. One of the Queen's great pleasures was that at Broadlands she was left in peace.

One morning Mandy had been to her ballet class and the Barratts told her she must stay indoors because the Queen was at the stables.

'What difference does that make?' the little girl wanted to know and, still wearing her tutu, managed to slip out and hide in the stables until the Queen arrived. Then, in a tutu that was by now somewhat grubby, she suddenly popped out and made a perfect bob. Somewhat startled, Her Majesty laughed and said: 'That was the nicest curtsey I have ever seen.'

'See,' said a triumphant Mandy afterwards. 'She didn't mind a bit!'

John Barratt's experience of Princess Anne was that she, too, was invariably warm and kind – and that she did herself no favours when she said she really did not care for children all that much. The Princess was always very good with his. Even when Mandy stared hard at her in the stable-yard one day and with the careless honesty of childhood said: 'What a funny hat you're wearing', Anne's reaction was to roar with laughter. But then, it was a funny hat.

Charles is enchanted by the things children do. An imaginative child once sent him a drawing of the Prince of Wales as a whale. He was greatly delighted with it and had it framed and hung. The young artist would no doubt be pleased to learn that this is more than he does with his own water-colours. He just leaves them lying around. The least vain of men, he does not always feel that they are good enough to frame.

There must be a million miles of film of Prince Charles but he dislikes seeing himself on screen. The only video of himself he ever watched over and over was of his two rides on Good Prospect and Alibar, the horse that died under him. And then only to see what mistakes he had made. He did manage to sit through a video of his wedding. He and his new bride watched it on the Royal Yacht while they were on their honeymoon. 'It is amazing how much you miss while it's all going on,' he said afterwards.

When he is being filmed or making a speech – sometimes off the cuff but more usually from notes – his Equerry will record him. Back at the Palace, one of the secretaries transcribes the tape and, with the transcript in front of him, he then listens to himself on tape, working to perfect his ability to speak in public. Anyone who watched his film on modern British architecture will appreciate that this method has taught him a great deal.

Charles has a particularly strong human side. All his closest friends know of his habit of nodding off. He will take cat naps in the car and he also frequently falls asleep over dinner. Those who entertain him are quite used to it. The usual routine is for the hostess to keep on talking as if he were awake. Then his eyes snap open and he's back to chatting normally again.

Like the rest of the human race he gets terrible colds, a problem that his son, Harry, seems to have inherited. Colds make the Prince thoroughly miserable. He takes to his bed and won't see anybody. He is basically a good-tempered man, more likely to heave a deep resigned sigh than shout at anyone, but he can get angry. When he is travelling and staying in hotels, there are four things that really annoy him: the noise of plumbing; the hiss and drip of an air conditioner; not being able to open windows because they are sealed; and miserable little towels – 'I will need six of these to bloody dry myself,' he grumbles. 'Can't someone *arrange* these things!' he pleads if everything does not come up to scratch.

He simply cannot abide smoking. There are no ash-trays in his homes, and those in his cars are kept firmly closed. He once had an Equerry who smoked strong French cigarettes. The unfortunate man spent his life sneaking down to the back of aircraft or into empty corridors for a quick puff, but the Prince always complained that he could still smell the smoke. About the only other thing that does drive him to distraction is being kept waiting, and wasting time. In this he takes after his father but there is no shouting in the Prince Philip fashion.

Princess Anne, who does shout, is undoubtedly her father's favourite, but then she is a classic chip off the old block. When Prince Philip was talking about his children he said that Anne had a lot of his own abrupt directness and practicality. In times of trouble Prince Philip is her staunch defender. In 1985, Anne's personal detective, Sergeant Peter Cross, was busy telling the press about his relationship with the Princess. It was a trying time for her. Prince Philip sent his daughter a short note. He said that he had heard what was being said and added with the loving simplicity of a truly kind father: 'Take care of yourself.' Peter Cross had been fired for over-familarity, protesting that it wasn't at all one-sided. Gradually the gossip died away.

Prince Philip's second favourite is Andrew, and again they have a great deal in common. When Andrew sprayed paint over the pursuing press on a visit to the USA he was merely copying an escapade of his father who, when younger, turned a hose on to cameramen in London. And yet, though undoubtedly macho, Andrew, to Prince Philip's disappointment, is not particularly sporty. In the days before his marriage, it was Andrew who kept Buckingham Palace open at the weekends entertaining his friends (much to the staff's chagrin who had to keep the place going just for him). While he was entertaining, the rest of the family took to the country. Perhaps Philip's biggest disappointment is that his youngest son, Edward, is neither particularly sporty nor at all macho.

Of his daughters-in-law, he is fondest of forthright Fergie, having less in common with the once shy Di. Not that shy Di was ever as timid as people thought. She did not whisper when she spoke. Right from the start she had both character and strong opinions, and was keenly observant. And although the Queen terrified her at first, she soon learned to stand on her own two feet. She tried hard to be independent from the word go. She is a lady who likes her own way. 'Freedom' was the cry. The insistence on freedom in the early days of marriage had her back in South Kensington almost every morning to see her former hairdresser, Kevin Shanley, at his salon, Headlines. That soon changed. She now appreciates that real freedom is relaxing in the bath for ten minutes longer and letting the hairdresser come to you. These days she enjoys the limelight but avoids poring over her press-cuttings. What she doesn't see doesn't hurt her and the sackful of letters soon lets her know public opinion, which was more puzzled than censorious, for example, when she once got a bad fit of the giggles in public.

Not surprisingly, in the early days she was under the most enormous nervous strain, but the Royals were wonderfully kind to her, appreciating that she was so young and vulnerable to the new pressures. On one occasion she got so fed-up with photographers while she tried to watch Charles play polo, that she burst into tears and rushed away. It was just before the wedding, and when she got home she was fussed and babied and made to go upstairs and rest.

Under normal circumstances to burst into tears like that would be absolutely the most unforgivable thing she could have done. Royalty never cry in public. Not even at the funerals of those they love. Nobody ever said a cross word to Diana, but it was the first and last time that she ever shed a tear in public – though sometimes there is a little bit of weeping back home where no one can see.

This insistence on a stiff upper lip is a comparatively modern hazard for royals. The family's Hanoverian ancestors were great weepers and wailers and would cry their eyes out – and publicly at that – if simply seeing a relative off on an overseas trip. The Georgians did not have to compete with the same huge batteries of media cameras of course, and the Press were much more respectful.

As recently as King George VI's funeral, BBC TV – without even being asked – cut out a shot of Queen Mary wiping away a mother's tear.

One major hazard is security. This might be easier for everyone concerned to bear if Prince Philip were not almost pathologically opposed to policemen. He does not like being able to see them, which makes their lives very difficult. He did, however, become a little more tolerant of their presence after Michael Fagan, a disturbed young man, broke into the Palace, and had to be evicted from the Queen's bedroom in the early morning.

All the Royal Family have the same curious quirk of seeming to believe that Sunday is safe. Sunday is a private day in their eyes, and therefore nothing untoward should happen. The Queen likes to drive herself to church at Windsor, and various members of the family drive themselves to Smith's Lawn for the polo in the afternoon. This occasion could not be more public and yet this is the time when Prince Philip is most adamant that he doesn't want to lay eyes on a policeman. Commander Michael Trestrail (who left Royal service after becoming involved in a homosexual scandal) had even more problems when he was put in charge of Royal security arrangements. He owned a bright orange station wagon. 'If he is going to stay,' said the Queen frostily, 'he will have to change that.' Orange is not a colour that pleases her.

The car was also far too conspicuous and wisely Trestrail changed it for a brown Rover. But as far as Prince Philip was concerned, the Commander himself was also too conspicuous. The poor fellow spent his first weeks at Smith's Lawn desperately trying to keep an eye on his Royal charges without being seen himself. Eventually, they came to accept him as a helpful and sadly necessary part of the surroundings. In fact, when, much against the Queen's will, he was forced to leave their service, all the Royal Family with the exception of Prince Philip wrote to him thanking him for the years of hard work that he had put in on their behalf.

When it comes to security, Prince Charles is philosophical about the dangers and has stated firmly that if he should ever be kidnapped, no one is to bow to the kidnappers' demands. He has ordered that no ransom money is to be paid merely because he happens to be the Prince of Wales. There have been times when the Special Branch have known that he is on an IRA target list. The Prince's attitude to this unwelcome news is fatalistic. Remembering the murder in Ireland of Uncle 'Dickie' Mountbatten, he says that if it is going to happen it will happen. He is always careful, though. When he drives himself he always keeps a sharp eye in the mirror for any car that looks as if it might be following him. And all Royal private homes are well equipped with panic buttons. They mostly look like pretty little boxes – but when pressed the noise is enough to wake the dead.

The Royals are just like any family with their likes and dislikes. The Queen Mother has her family favourites. Of her grandchildren, Prince Charles will always be first in her affections, but these days Lady Sarah Armstrong-Jones, too, has found herself a niche in the Queen Mother's heart. And though she and Princess Anne never had a great rapport, possibly because Anne was so much her father's girl, she is deeply fond of young Peter Philips. She can't abide the German relations, as they are known in the family. These are Prince Philip's sisters and their husbands and children who make regular and totally unpublicised visits to Britain, and whose existence is kept very quiet from the British public. Prince Philip and Prince Charles visit them in Germany, but with some secrecy. When he was younger, Philip would go boar hunting on their vast estates. And they always come to England for the Windsor Horse Show in May. But no song and dance is made about their visits, even today, so long after the war. It is odd to think that Prince Charles has fourteen German first cousins who are never mentioned in Britain.

But the German relations have always been a bit of an embarrassment. Prince Philip had four sisters, and all of them married high-ranking, wealthy Germans. One sister died in a plane crash before the Second World War. Two married dedicated Nazis. One of these, a bomber pilot, paid London an unwelcome visit or two, but died in action over Italy. The fourth sister married the Margrave of Baden who, before the war, ran Salem School – the German equivalent of Gordonstoun. Philip was sent there as a teenager but once the school fell under Nazi influence his brother-in-law very sensibly sent him to Britain for his own safety. Philip had a habit of mocking the Hitler salute. Having been to an English prep school, to him the upraised hand meant permission to leave the room for a call of nature.

It is hardly surprising, therefore, that when Prince Philip married the future Queen of England so soon after the war, his sisters and their controversial husbands were not invited to the wedding. It might have been diplomatic, but it was hard on Philip and hard on them, for they were close as children.

In a turn-up for the book, Prince Charles quite likes Princess Diana's step-mother, the Countess of Spencer. Probably much to his wife's annoyance. Diana took him to her family home Althorp after the engagement, and Prince Charles was most amused by the outrageous Countess who even calls the butler 'Darling'. She had laid on a great 'do' for the weekend – hiring a pianist from the Savoy (who appeared a night too early and had to come back again), and was determined to make it all a huge success. It was all done very stylishly and in the grand manner with candles and dinner dress in the superb setting of Althorp which is really rather grander than any of the Queen's private homes – though it does not match Windsor Castle. Prince Charles enjoyed himself immensely. Princess Diana couldn't wait to get away.

Princess Margaret deeply disapproves of Princess Michael because she is a Catholic. Perhaps there is also some resentment because Princess Michael, a divorced woman, was allowed to marry into the Royal Family while Princess Margaret had to renounce the love of her life, Peter Townsend, because he had been divorced.

The feeling, however, is mutual and although they are near-neighbours at Kensington Palace the two Princesses seldom see each other unless they have to. Princess Michael, once described as 'a woman who, in her life, has had two husbands and three accents', is a strong and positive character. Born in Middle Europe, she shed that accent when her family emigrated to Australia after the war, and the Australian accent was lost when she first came to Britain and married Tom Trowbridge, a well-to-do banker. After almost seven years the marriage was annulled in 1978. Her emotional European ways and outspoken interviews have made her a sitting target for the media who have accused her of almost everything from having a Nazi father to having an affair with a wealthy member of a Texan oil family.

In a bizarre sequence of events, all secretly monitored by the Press, she was reputed to have darted between an Eton Square apartment where her friend Ward Hunt was staying, and her Kensington Palace home where her husband Prince Michael was staying, wearing a series of disguises including a long red wig.

Because no member of the Royal Family ever replies to Press speculation, nothing was said officially but Princess Michael advised Ward Hunt to return to Dallas as quickly as he could.

In the world of the Royals the aftermath was quite predictable. While the media published almost every detail of the alleged romance, Princess Michael was busy being seen out with her husband and behaving towards him in a most 'lovey-dovey' manner. The Royal Family closed ranks, doggedly presenting a bland, united and silent front, behaving as if absolutely nothing had occurred. The Queen, who is exceedingly fond of her cousin,

Prince Michael, was determined to calm the situation and make it appear as if nothing was amiss. Princess Michael was made more welcome for a while within the family circle.

The Queen did the same for Major Ronald Ferguson, Fergie's father and Prince Charles's polo manager, who caused the Royal Family embarrassment when he was discovered to be patronising a West End massage parlour. He was photographed arriving and leaving and then the girls who gave their supposedly 'discreet massages' spoke to the Press about their experiences with the Major and several other celebrity clients including Cabinet ministers, actors and aristocrats. The story escalated into a huge scandal and eventually the fifty-six-year-old Major lost his job as Deputy Chairman of the exclusive Guards Polo Club. He also lost some of his friends, but not the Queen and Prince Charles. The Prince of Wales is very close to the outspoken Major and stayed by his side. Princess Diana vowed to boycott polo matches at the Guards Club in future as a gesture of support – as did his daughter, the Duchess of York.

'The advice I had at the time,' the Major explained, 'was to hold my head up, carry on with my work and say nothing. And that is what I did.'

The Major's son-in-law, Prince Andrew, also had the misfortune to tangle with women who 'kissed-and-told'. Long before he was involved with Sarah Ferguson, the intimate details of his love life, as told by former model Vicki Hodge, were splashed all over the front pages. It was not very dignified, but Prince Andrew was young and single and Prince Philip has always believed it better for his sons to sow their wild oats while young. Vicki Hodge broke the rules in talking. She is now busy penning her autobiography in which she will no doubt talk again. On the handsome proceeds of selling the original story to a Sunday newspaper, she settled in Barbados. The matter upset many people and Miss Hodge particularly incurred the wrath of her sister, Wendy, who happens to be married to one of Prince Charles' polo-playing cronies, Johnny Kidd. Publicly, the Royal Family completely ignored the newspapers reports. Privately, they caused many a wry smile. Word was that, back at the Palace, Andrew was in hot water with his father for being stupid enough to get involved with an indiscreet woman who had sold stories about her previous lovers to the newspapers.

Prince Charles and Prince Andrew do not get on all that well. Andrew regards Charles as being rather stuffy. Charles thinks of his brother as a bit of a tearaway. One Christmas when Andrew was having romantic problems he was refusing to buy presents for the family or even send a card. The Queen, who loves Christmas and all the ritual of presents and cards, was dismayed.

In desperation, she asked Prince Charles to have a word with his brother. With some reluctance, he did, but getting no response came away from the meeting muttering, 'I give up!'

In the event, however, big brother Charles had more influence than he realised. Later that afternoon Andrew was seen running round the shops of Windsor, his detective puffing behind, as the Prince did a bit of last-minute Christmas shopping!

There has always been speculation as to whether the Princess of Wales and the Princess Royal get along. The answer is yes, but that they have nothing in common. Diana herself will never quite fit comfortably into the family mould of huntin', shootin', and fishin'.

Rumours that they dislike each other began in 1982 when Princess Anne was on an official visit to the United States and Princess Diana was heavily pregnant. Anne was asked by a reporter, 'Has your Royal Highness any word about Princess Diana?'

Princess Anne snapped back, 'I don't know. You tell me.'

She was not slighting Diana, she was putting down the Press. The Royals consider it extremely bad form for anyone to make enquiries about the well-being of other members of their family. Or indeed of themselves. People meeting the Queen Mother are told firmly not to comment either on her age or how well she looks. But, of course, while Anne was probably in the right she made the mistake of reacting in a sourpuss fashion. Had the Queen Mother been asked the same question she may well have given the same answer – but it would have been delivered with grace and charm.

After Prince Charles and Lady Diana married, Anne did show touches of jealousy towards her sister-in-law. It was after the wedding when it began to look as if Diana's popularity was pushing the Queen's daughter out into the cold that attention was paid to Anne's work. After years of surly behaviour and grumbles from critics that she never did anything to earn her Civil List money, suddenly she was portrayed as being the hardest-working Royal of them all, and heartily deserved the title of the Princess Royal. The fact that she had decided to keep her position in the Royal hierarchy became clear when the Royal Regiment wanted to appoint a new Colonel-in-Chief. Their previous Colonel-in-Chief had been the late Princess Royal. The regiment were rather keen for Princess Diana to take the role. It went to Princess Anne and long before the Queen appointed her Princess Royal.

The Princesses Diana and Anne are near neighbours. Their

homes Highgrove and Gatcombe Park in 'Royal' Gloucestershire are only ten miles apart. But they are not particularly neighbourly. Nor is there much traffic between the two houses. Princess Diana is often there for children's parties and when Anne is away she will pop over to make sure that Anne's children, Zara and Peter, are not missing their mother too much. Anne has never taken her children anywhere publicly.

People forget that there is an eleven-year age gap between Anne and Diana and apart from family they haven't much to talk about. Anne is crazy about horses. Horses frighten Diana. Diana relaxes by embroidering cushions while Anne prefers something active like helping her husband around the farm. Diana adores clothes and shopping, both of which bore Anne.

On a visit to Australia the Press complained that she was wearing a suit which she had worn on a previous visit in 1978.

'Oh, it's much older than that,' said Anne cheerfully.

Anne has grit and guts. At home and abroad she works harder than anyone else in the Royal Family. And to her own surprise she has found that she is now popular. She could end up being the most popular Princess of all – if for some reason Diana drops out of the public eye.

But Anne is the odd one out. Her home is run in a most unroyal manner. The butler complains that it is open house for everyone. Girl grooms in jeans and wellington boots are in and out of the house – something that is not permitted in any other Royal home. The Queen has been to Gatcombe Park only a few times, perhaps because of lack of time in her busy life, and perhaps because Anne's casual, country style and complete absence of protocol could cause problems with that endless need to maintain the dignity of the Monarchy. Added to which, the Queen simply cannot bear mess and muddle.

In spite of the green wellingtons all over the place, and Anne in her jeans and funny hats, Gatcombe Park is still a very fine house for a farming family. It was bought in 1976, from Lord Butler, the late Conservative MP, Rab Butler. It cost around £750,000, which for the entire estate worked out at £1,000 an acre.

Who, however, bought Gatcombe Park? Why mum, Her Majesty the Queen, of course, just as she will pay for the Duke and Duchess of York's ranch-style house in Sunninghill, near Windsor. Both houses were bought with monies from trust funds set up by the Queen when the children were small.

Fergie and Anne get on quite well – better, in fact, than Diana and Anne. They have a lot more in common and Anne feels sympathy with Fergie's present state of unpopularity. She also feels Andrew does little to help his wife apart from fuelling the fire with inane remarks such as those he made at Lockerbie after a Pan Am jet was blown up, plunging onto the town. He was unwise enough to say, 'What I have seen will leave a lasting impression . . . It's very sad for the town but my deepest feelings go out to the people, the families of those Americans who died in the crash. I feel more strongly for these people.'

The remarks were meant to come from the heart, but sounded trite and insensitive, and as far as Anne was concerned it was another occasion when her thick-skinned younger brother had bungled. She was not the only person to feel this. You would have thought that he would have been more sensitive about *our* feelings, the people of the devastated Scottish town complained.

Fergie it seems, has to carry the burden for both of them and it is not easy.

A naturally lively and enthusiastic person, Sarah Ferguson was everyone's darling when she first became engaged to Prince Andrew. Nobody minded that she had a past – had lived with an older man and mixed with a *louche*, fast set. They didn't mind that, unlike Princess Diana, her figure was not that of a model, and they didn't care that she wasn't the daughter of a Duke or an Earl. She was natural, tactile and caring and approached her Royal duties with a refreshing, relaxed attitude. Possibly too relaxed, too co-operative and too eager to please. Fergie began to suffer the same fate of nearly all new recruits to the 'Royal firm'. Continual criticism: her face, her hair and above all her clothes and 'freebie' holidays were under constant attack.

'Of course, she does not like criticism,' her father said, coming to her defence, 'but as I explained to her, she is no longer a private person. She is a public person now.'

Fergie the private person and Fergie the public person were at odds with each other. She cannot understand why she is the recipient of so much negative press. But as the distinguished writer, Bernard Levin once said, 'For a reason I do not fully understand, there has to be, at any time, one bad royal. The choice is entirely arbitrary and bears no relation at all to the personal qualities or conduct of the chosen victim. The attacks on the Duchess of York are entirely impersonal.'

Before Fergie it was Princess Michael the public loved to hate, and before her, Princess Anne. Today the Princess Royal is voted the most hard-working member of the Royal Family and is almost treated as a saint for her tireless work for the Save the Children

Fund. The same swing in the popularity polls will almost certainly come to the Duchess of York once her time of trial is over.

The Queen is acutely aware of the hurt that adverse publicity can cause her family and does her best to help. Constant speculation that the marriage of Princess Anne and Captain Mark Phillips was on the rocks may have filled mountainous miles of newspaper columns, but the Royal family strove to appear all was well. In the end, it was the public humiliating of Mark Phillips that finished the marriage.

Mark had gritted his teeth and made little comment through the 1985 revelations of his wife's extraordinary friendship with her policeman, Peter Cross. Even after the passionate policeman was sacked for "overfamiliarity," probably at Mark's instigation, Cross and the Princess still met. The public may have forgotten Sergeant Cross, but Mark could not.

Early in 1989, Princess Anne gained her mother's reluctant permission for a separation. Mark was to realize it was the only answer when, in April of 1989, he learned—from reading newspaper stories!—that affectionate letters written to his wife by the Queen's equerry, Commander Tim Laurence, had been stolen.

By the end of August, all the legal details had been worked out and the separation officially announced. In this instance, the Queen, who adores her daughter, had little choice but to act on Anne's behalf.

The Queen is a staunch supporter of her newest daughter-in-law, the Duchess of York, as well.

'Sarah can twist the Queen around her little finger,' friends say. 'The Queen is totally supportive, but when she gives advice she expects Sarah to take note.'

Unfortunately, Sarah doesn't always listen. It was said that the Queen advised her not to leave baby Beatrice behind again and go on another ski-ing holiday. She still went. When she came back, she did buckle down to work; perhaps the Queen had told Andrew to keep as low a profile as possible and let his wife carry out most of the Royal duties while he stuck to his Naval ones. The Queen is delighted with the influence Fergie has had on her son since their marriage.

'Andrew,' friends confirm, 'who can be so grand and regal, is a pussycat around Sarah. She has loosened him up, calmed him down and brought out a side to him we never knew he had. Why, he's even stopped laughing at his own jokes.'

# Magic Childhood

One aspect of Royal life that has changed amazingly in three generations is childhood. The Queen's own father was confined to the nursery all day and every day, except between the hours of five and six when he and his brothers and sister were dressed up and brought downstairs to see their parents. 'Bertie', as the family called him, was the second son and a sickly child. His first nanny disliked him. She treated him with great cruelty until his parents discovered what was happening and the woman was summarily sent packing. But much damage had already been done not only to the young Duke of York's self-confidence but his delicate health as well. His troubles were perpetuated by an education which strove to correct his left-handness and only succeeded in giving him a stammer. These childhood disasters affected him for the rest of his life. He was shy, nervous and continued to be disposed to ill-health. But in the final analysis, a colossal effort of will and the loving support of his wife, Elizabeth, produced for both Britain and distant lands a truly fine and much-loved King.

Perhaps because his own early days had been so miserable, he ensured that his children, the Princesses Elizabeth and Margaret, had a magic childhood. They were brought up in the traditional Royal manner with nannies, a governess and little contact with the outside world, and their doting, loving parents selected with great care those who were to have a hand in bringing up their children. Their mother had the greatest confidence in their nanny, Mrs Clara Knight. With good reason. Mrs Knight had been nanny to the

Duchess of York when she and her brother David were babies. Elizabeth and Margaret were pretty, happy children who adored their parents, their nanny (whom they called Allah) their maids, Bobo and Ruby Macdonald, and Crawfie (Marion Crawford) their governess. For them, childhood was a lyrical time. But it was disrupted by two events of great significance – the abdication of Edward VIII, which put their father on the throne, and the outbreak of the Second World War which meant that they, like so many other children of the period, had to be separated from their parents. While their mother and father stayed in London, Elizabeth and Margaret Rose went to the comparative safety of Windsor.

Even today the most private area of the Queen's life is her role as a mother and grandmother. Few people realise what a great disappointment it was to her that she was not able to have her planned family of four in a shorter time. When the unexpected death of her father catapulted her to the throne, she was a twenty-five-year-old wife and mother. Prince Charles and Princess Anne were four and two respectively and saw comparatively little of their mother. Even before she became Queen, her father's ill-health was putting an increasing burden on her already busy public life.

For those first years the duties of a Monarch made it impossible for her to increase her family. It was only when she was secure on the throne that she and Prince Philip decided that a ten-year gap between what was to be their first and second families was quite wide enough. And along came Prince Andrew in 1960 with Edward following four years later.

The two youngest members of the family were able to enjoy their mother's company more than had been possible for Prince Charles and Princess Anne. When Andrew and Edward were very small, and their nanny, Mabel Anderson, went out to her pottery classes in the evening or to dinner with friends who lived outside the Palace, the Queen would baby-sit her two youngest sons. Her Page and footman would serve her a light supper at the nursery table, and she would spend the evening quite content, watching the nursery TV until Nanny Anderson returned.

Even when she was at her busiest, she always tried to be in the nursery when it came to bathtime for all her children, to rub them dry and give them a kiss and cuddle before bed.

When she came to the throne, Winston Churchill was her Prime Minister and she asked if the time of the Tuesday evening audience could be changed from 5.30 to 6.30 so as not to upset the nursery hour. The sentimental Winston was delighted to oblige and the hour has never been changed back throughout the terms of seven subsequent prime ministers, including that of Margaret Thatcher.

Prince Charles was the first heir to the throne to be sent to school, and for this little guinea pig it was misery. Friends recommended Hill House in London's Knightsbridge. It was and still is run by the affable Colonel Townsend who, after taking tea with the Queen agreed that Charles should attend for afternoons only to start with and continue morning lessons with his governess, Miss Peebles. It was Autumn term, 1956. The following January, eight-year-old Charles started attending full time, and on his first day the school was surrounded by pressmen. This made his new venture even more painful for the introverted, sensitive Charles. His first day was an ordeal. Not only did he have all the unwelcome attention, but his beloved Nanny, Helen Lightbody, was retired from royal service and he missed her very much. For years afterwards he used to visit her at her 'grace and favour flat' in Kennington, in South London, and when she died in 1987, aged seventy-nine, he sent a hand-written note, 'For Nana, in loving memory of early childhood' which was attached to a wreath.

Surprisingly, he presented his young son Prince William with an almost identical set of circumstances when William first went to school in January 1987. When the little Prince returned from his first day at Wetherby School in Notting Hill he discovered that HIS beloved nanny, Barbara Barnes, was also leaving royal service. It was a great blow to both him and his young brother, Harry.

William was not in the least alarmed by school. Harry, when his turn came, was not so sure, but at least William was there to give him confidence. For Charles it was all much more traumatic. Prince Philip took the misguided view that Charles's lack of brilliance and natural shyness would not impede him in any way at school and he was determined the young Prince should follow in father's footsteps. So at the age of nine Charles was sent off, full of fears and gloom, to his father's old preparatory school – Cheam. Lacking his father's assertive boisterousness he was always the odd one out. He was the boy who always had detectives hovering and the boy who brought unwelcome Press attention to the school. Everyone knew that his mother was the Queen. The other children were either sycophantic or hostile. Later he went on to Gordonstoun where Philip, blunt, unacademic and self-sufficient, had spent a happy, energetic and sporting youth. Charles loathed the place. His introverted and artistic temperament were at odds with the unconventional school. He had a schoolboy dream that he could

*Above* Prince Charles, aged three, squeezes his sister Anne's hand. He was an affectionate child and during this photographic session was asked to kiss his sister. His enthusiasm was such that he embraced her too hard and she burst into tears. *(Alpha)*

*Right* Ever since Bobo Macdonald who looked after the young Princess Elizabeth, the Royal Family have had a liking for Scottish staff. Here Nurse Helen Lightbody holds the infant Princess Anne. Nanny's uniform in the fifties was plain, but always included a hat and gloves. *(Alpha)*

*Below* Nanny and children on the Royal Yacht Britannia accompanied by Prince Philip's mother, Princess Andrew of Greece in the nun's habit. *(Alpha)*

*Left* The latest addition to the Royal Family. Princess Beatrice is unbuckled from her pram by uniformed nanny, Alison Wardley, while Fergie prepares to meet her husband. *(Alpha)*

*Below* The paternal Duke of York carries his daughter down the gangplank of his ship, *HMS Edinburgh*. To the delight of the crowd she appears to be waving. *(Glenn Harvey Collection)*

*Left* Royal children have plenty of playmates amongst their immediate family and here Prince William is seen with his favourite cousin, Zara, Princess Anne and Captain Mark Phillips' daughter. *(Glenn Harvey Collection)*

*Below left* Prince Edward was closest to Princess Margaret's daughter, Lady Sarah Armstrong-Jones; seen here at Victoria Station in the early seventies. *(Alpha)*

*Below right* Still friends, Edward and Sarah walk together to church nearly twenty years later. *(Glenn Harvey Collection)*

*Right* The Queen with her grandson, Prince Harry leaving church. Dressed in their smartest clothes, Royal children are introduced to regular church outings as soon as they are old enough to sit still. *(Glenn Harvey Collection)*

*Above* Charles and Anne in the early sixties. Anne was the more competitive of the two children and inherited much of her father's toughness. Charles, more like his mother, had a great sense of humour and an inherent sense of duty from a very early age. *(Alpha)*

*Right* The Queen demonstrates how to divest oneself of too many flowers to one of her Ladies-in-Waiting, Lady Farnham. *(Alpha)*

*Left* Prince William, a fearless rider, is seen here preparing to be led over some quite large jumps, while competing in a local gymkhana in Gloucestershire. *(Alpha)*

*Left* Prince Harry, a little more reluctant than his elder brother, surveys the scene from comparative safety behind his pony's head. *(Alpha)*

*Above* Princess Anne has found a new challenge in race riding. A dangerous and competitive sport, she is fit enough and good enough to have done well in spite of several nasty falls. *(Glenn Harvey Collection)*

*Above* Prince Charles on his 40th birthday in November 1988. Being embraced by an admirer on one side and interviewed on the other was all part of the tremendous enthusiasm which greeted his birthday celebrations in the North of England. *(Alpha)*

*Top right* Prince Charles was back on the ski slopes of Klosters a year after the tragic avalanche which killed Major Hugh Lindsay. Next to him is ski guide, Bruno Sprecher. *(Glenn Harvey Collection)*

*Below* The Prince of Wales grimaces in mock horror as he eases himself out of a tank during a visit to one of his many regiments. *(Glenn Harvey Collection)*

*Above* The late Earl Mountbatten of Burma escorts his favourite nephew, the young Prince Charles. Mountbatten had a strong influence on the Prince, who still misses him ten years after his assassination. *(Alpha)*

*Right* The Prince and Princess of Wales are rarely photographed together for they both have such busy schedules they prefer to work individually. However, for social events like Royal Ascot they enjoy themselves with their mutual friends. *(Alpha)*

*Left* Princess Diana, whose ravishing looks and gentle nature win her many admirers, is seen here making polite conversation during a tour of Dubai. *(Alpha)*

*Below* Dissolved in laughter, the Princess had just caught sight of the most outrageous hat in the Royal Enclosure at Ascot. *(Alpha)* run away and hide in the forest and never be found. He hated going back to school after holidays and eventually confided his unhappiness to his grandmother, the Queen Mother. She put on one of her marvellous hats and went to see him; she talked to him and gave him strengthened heart to carry on.

She would have preferred Charles to go to Eton where her brothers and most of her family friends and advisors had been educated. It was right on her Royal Lodge doorstep and she considered it so 'suitable'. The Queen, too, veered towards choosing Eton, but Philip had his way as, in family matters, he always has.

Both Charles and Diana hated going to boarding school. The Princess has said that there were many tears when she was sent away. So what will this doting mother do about William and Harry? Will she let Prince Charles do as his father did, and send his boys to Cheam and Gordonstoun? Or will it this time be Eton where the Spencer men were educated? Prince Charles has said that the children will not follow in his footsteps without considerable thought. Before a final decision is made the Prince will no doubt visit his old schools again. Much will have changed and it is possible that he might not agree with the changes.

Diana says that William is the worry. If he is the first one in the family to do something different he will have to bear the brunt of it all. But if William likes the outdoor life, as many members of the Royal Family do, she and Charles will pick on a school which reflects that. (Gordonstoun could then be a contender again.) Both parents feel it would be exceedingly difficult for William or Harry to attend a State day school because of the overwhelming security problems and the fact that there would be no respite from the media. It will, therefore, almost certainly be boarding school. This will be a wrench for Diana. 'The best part of my day is getting home to the children,' she always says.

At one time the Princess was toying with the idea of setting up a nursery school at Kensington Palace. After all, she had had excellent experience working in a kindergarten before she married. With a nursery school at hand, safe from Press intrusion, her sons would be spared the problems the shy young Prince of Wales suffered when he first went to Hill House. They could learn, painlessly, to relate to other children. But the idea bit the dust, probably from a lack of other children to invite. Playmates are always in short supply for Princes.

William and Harry's uncles, Prince Andrew and Prince Edward, were more fortunate. When they were small there was something of a boom in Royal babies. Princess Margaret had her two, David and Sarah, and George and Helen of Kent were small children, along with Princess Alexandra's James and Marina. All the children were much of an age. The nurseries at Balmoral, Windsor and Sandringham were alive and well. Now with the birth of Princess Beatrice, they will no doubt come into their own again.

It is obviously difficult for Royal children when they are sent to school. They can never know if a hand of friendship is offered merely because of their position, while other children may shyly back away, making them feel isolated. Their schoolmates are uncertain how to behave, and the Royal children themselves learn prematurely who they are. Some people feel there is a risk of them getting a too great a sense of their position, before they are able to cope with the knowledge that they really are rather special.

Prince Charles, who even as a child never knew how to begin to show off, rarely gave any indication that he understood his rank. There was an occasion when he was eight years old and had been invited to have lunch with his grandmother at Royal Lodge. He went alone. His sister Anne was in bed with a cold. As the limousine arrived at Victoria Tower at Windsor Castle to pick him up, he asked his father, 'Please can I ride in the back on my own this time? You know, daddy, like a Prince.'

Prince Philip agreed that he could, and the Queen Mother, waiting to greet him, remarked that he had arrived in style. 'Yes, Granny, I thought I'd travel like a Prince this time,' he told her solemnly.

This sudden realization that he knew he was special was sharply marked by this incident because hitherto, like any small boy would, he had pestered to be allowed to sit in the front passenger seat alongside the chauffeur. And as for his mother being the Monarch, as far as he was concerned her main claim to fame was that she was 'Queen of all the soldiers'. In her younger years the Queen, too, had her rare moments of grandeur. Out with her grandmother, Queen Mary, one day, a footman lifted her down from a carriage saying, 'Come along then, little lady.' Said the future Queen, all hauteur, 'I am not a lady. I am a Princess.'

'And one day,' said her grandmother tartly, 'we hope you will be a lady as well.'

Prince William could do with a Queen Mary in his life. He is known as Billy Basher at school and if thwarted threatens the other boys with dire retribution when he is King. 'My daddy is the Prince of Wales and he can beat up your daddy,' he boasts, 'and when I'm King I'm going to send my knights round to kill you.'

There is a touch of Just William about the little Prince. He is a

28

small tornado, swift at pulling things apart, and with enough energy to wear out a prize fighter. Prince Charles on being presented with toys for his first born has been heard to mutter, 'William will make short work of that!'

Charles, who was basically such a solemn little boy, must wonder where the destructive streak comes from, particularly as Princess Diana, though naughty, was never wild. She was a gentle little girl, always trying to help the smaller children.

No doubt the couple tell themselves that he gets it from Prince Andrew, or Princess Anne, or even Princess Margaret – all three of whom were holy terrors when young. The Royal Family has always had its share of little rebels.

Millions of other families all over the world have their own versions of young William. The only difference is that the Prince and his little brother, Harry, are the first Royal children so near to the throne who stand a very good chance of being thoroughly spoilt.

It was Princess Diana, thwarted in her desire for a Palace nursery school, who broke with protocol in sending young William and Harry to Mrs Mynors' nursery school in Notting Hill Gate. They are the first Royal children not to be taught at home by a Governess until going to prep school at eight. The extrovert William thoroughly enjoys school. Prince Harry, more like his father in character, is not so content. It is said that he is withdrawn and nervous.

There was a lot of opposition to the Princess' plan mainly because the problems of security were so horrendous, and because the little Princes' playmates were going to have to get used to a couple of policemen hanging around all the time. But Diana was determined. The parents of William's classmates may wish that she had lost the battle. The lad has a formidable personality. He tried once to flush a pair of shoes down the lavatory – without success. Although he had much better luck with a classmate's lunch snack.

Royal children are pretty much like anyone's children when it comes to naughtiness. Princess Anne spotted early on that the Palace sentries went through the noisy routine of presenting arms every time she passed. It didn't take long before she was walking past them deliberately – until she found herself standing to attention in front of her Governess, Miss Peebles, who had noticed what was going on. All Royal children like to make their detectives run. The Queen and Princess Margaret were always giving theirs the slip and making him pelt after them. Charles and Anne did the same. And when Charles and Anne were given boxing gloves as children, they tore into each other with such ferocity that their alarmed father took the gloves away.

A normal reaction between siblings one might say. But the future King wasn't much different from any small boy. Once when he and Anne were let out on their own in Ballater, the little town that serves Balmoral, they headed for a toy shop, clutching their pocket money. After long consideration the Princess bought a cupid's bow false lip and Prince Charles settled for a packet of sneezing powder!

His son, William, is behaving in pretty much the way that Prince Andrew used to when he was a small boy. Norman Myers, who as 'Uncle Myers' and his assistant, 'Monty the Monkey', have entertained two generations of Royal children, agrees. 'William is like Andrew was,' he says, 'extroverted and a bit cheeky. But a happy person and utterly delightful. Harry's more like Edward. More shy and introverted.'

Prince Andrew was such a nuisance that a long-suffering footman once thumped him and gave him a black eye. There must have been some sympathy for the footman, because not a word was said. On the other hand, Prince Philip once turned up at a film premiere sporting a black eye of his own. It had been inflicted by the highly-active young Andrew.

He was a rather physical child, and even as a young man prone to giving people hearty whacks around the shoulders. He bumped into a staff member who had once been a nursery footman when he and Edward were small.

'Hello!' said Andrew. (Bash around the shoulders.) 'How are you?' (Another bash around the shoulders.)

Prince Charles just happened to be walking by on his way to his rooms and saw what was going on. 'Andrew,' he commanded, 'stop hitting people.'

'But I've *always* hit him,' Andrew replied, all sweet reasonableness. And it was true. He had.

Andrew would pull both the corgis' tails and the footmen's coat tails. He would create havoc in the nursery and refuse to clear it up. Prince Charles, who took breakfast every morning in the nursery when the boys were small, would attempt to play the big brother. Andrew would take not one bit of notice. It was fortunate that Prince Edward was as good as gold. Two Andrews would be too much for any one nursery. But Nanny Anderson, who brought up all four of the Queen's children, adored Andrew and it was her contention that he would turn out to be the best of them in the end. Well, we shall see.

Shy Di was not always as well behaved as she might have us now believe. Her elder sister, Sarah, with Diana's help disposed of a string of nannies who eventually refused to put up with their naughtiness. Diana locked one of them in the bathroom and threw another's clothes out onto the roof. Now we know where William gets it from! But her worst fault was her impossible stubborness. She would not do anything that she did not wish to do. The girl was the embryo of the woman to come. She is still obstinate and which does little to oil the wheels of a happy marriage.

Fergie was better and the various nannies that were employed by her young parents at their house Lowood, in Sunninghill, near Ascot, remember her fondly. Ritva Risu from Finland recalls of the two sisters, Sarah and Jane, 'Sarah was always my favourite. She was just so good and gentle, even as a little girl. She was quiet as a mouse and once her head hit the pillow she was out like a light.'

Ritva, who slept in an adjoining bedroom to the two little girls, called Sarah 'My little redhair' in her broken English, and remembers that the child had a strong will. 'She had a strength of character about her,' she recalls.

It is hard to imagine the Queen being downright naughty as a child and she rarely was. She left the tantrums to Princess Margaret. But once, bored to death with French verbs, she picked up the ink-pot and put it upside down on her head. There sat the future Queen, black ink trickling down her face and dyeing her golden curls, waiting to see what her Governess was going to do about it. It turned out to be Nanny who was crosser as Nanny had to get the ink off.

Charles was the good child in the nursery; Anne the naughty one. But Charles was no angel. His grandmother used to take him to morning service when he was staying with her at Royal Lodge. He would sit through the lessons and hymns, but the sermon was more than he could bear and he would fidget, distracting everyone else. The Queen Mother took to taking him out before the sermon and then going back in herself.

He was easily distracted. At Buckingham Palace the nursery dining room was at one end of a kitchenette that looked out over the Mall. Intriguing noises from the outside world set Charles running to the window. The children were not permitted to leave table until they had finished eating, and these dashes to the window were dealt with sternly by Nanny Lightbody or her nursery assistant Mabel Anderson. A slap or a smacked bottom generally resulted. One suspects the same rules do not apply to William and Harry. Modern methods rule today as much in Royal Palaces as anywhere else.

Prince Charles escaped a smack on one occasion by keeping his mouth shut. In the nursery suite at Buckingham Palace there was a special bell which when rung meant that the Queen urgently wished to see Nurse Lightbody, the head Nanny. One day it rang and Miss Lightbody hurried down to the Queen's drawing-room. She knocked, entered when bidden, and said, 'You rang Your Majesty?' The Queen looked puzzled, smiled and shook her head.

Nurse Lightbody returned to the nursery and a few minutes later she was surprised to hear the bell ring again. She arrived back at the Queen's room to find her equally surprised. 'Do you think someone might be playing a joke on you?' the Queen asked.

Someone was. And Nanny Lightbody knew who when she came across Prince Charles innocently driving his pedal car along the Queen's corridor, not too far from the bell-push.

'Do you know what that's for?' she asked, pointing to the bell.

'Oh, yes,' said Charles, all innocence. 'When that rings you have to go and see mummy.'

'Only your mummy is supposed to ring it,' Nanny Lightbody said sternly. 'She would be cross if she caught someone else doing it.'

Prince Charles scuttled off. Later, Miss Lightbody discovered that he had been having a detailed conversation with the Palace electrician about which push rang which bell.

His son William did better. When he was just over a year old his Nanny, Barbara Barnes, made the mistake of leaving him unattended in the Balmoral nursery. She was only gone for a few seconds, but William discovered a bell on the wall and pushed it, thereby sending an urgent signal direct to the police headquarters in Aberdeen some fifty miles away. His experiment set off a full-scale red alert, bringing down both policemen and fire-engines in considerable strength. He was not popular.

Like his father before him, when he was nearly seven years old, Prince William fell in love with a striking little blonde a few months younger than him, named Eleanor Newton. She was a classmate at his old nursery school. Eleanor confessed, 'I just met Wills in our old classroom and he told me quite clearly that he was my boyfriend. He also told me that if I don't marry him he'll put me in his jail.'

This macho approach to the matter was not Prince Charles'

style at all at the same age. He was much more of a romantic. Charles met his first love at his Thursday afternoon dancing classes conducted by Miss Betty Vacani. Miss Vacani was something of a legend in Royal circles. She taught the Queen and Princess Margaret to dance and much later, by an amazing coincidence, employed Diana to teach two year olds and upwards to dance to nursery rhymes. Diana, having grown too tall to be a dancer herself, had decided to teach, but eventually abandoned the idea. As Miss Vacani delicately put it, 'She had rather a full social life.'

When the Queen was taught by Miss Vacani, boys were not allowed in the classes but by the time Charles was old enough to learn, times had changed. He turned out to be a natural dancer, even as a small boy. The classes were held at Buckingham Palace and he always made a bee-line for a very pretty little brunette called Julie Parker. (He went for blondes once he had grown up.) She was the daughter of Michael Parker, who was Private Secretary to Prince Philip. Julie was Charles' regular dancing partner among the other little children there, and he always asked if she could stay on for nursery tea. He was particularly attached to a particular dress she wore made of blue velvet with a butterfly on it, and when she didn't wear it he wanted to know where it was.

When Charles gave a children's party on his mother's Coronation Day, Julie was an honoured guest. The party took place in one of the rooms overlooking the Mall. Television sets were installed and boxes, covered with scarlet carpet, were put on the balcony so the children would be high enough to watch the parade below. A butler was in charge and there were five waiters to serve.

Prince Charles was always thrilled at the idea of seeing Julie, but the two children were parted when she went with her parents to Australia, as they were accompanying a Royal tour. Just before leaving she went to the dancing class and found it had been extended into a farewell party for her given by Charles and Anne.

After tea, as goodbyes were being said, Charles looked at Nurse Lightbody. 'May I kiss Julie goodbye?' he asked. Nanny laughed and said 'Yes,' and Charles solemnly kissed the little girl on the cheek.

'And now may I kiss her mama?' he asked and, when Charles had got his permission Mrs Parker bent down to receive her kiss.

When Julie went out of his life on that occasion, she left with his parents, and it was some weeks before he saw them again. There is always a public fuss when Royal children are left behind, but in fact, they get fairly blasé about being separated from their mothers and fathers. Nanny, the surrogate mother, is always there and the children accept early on that their parents have to go away. Shortly after the Queen's birth her parents set off on a tour of Australia and New Zealand and they did not see their baby again for six months. Jet travel did not exist. But there was no criticism from the public. The media were more respectful in those days. The new Duchess of York, however, came in for a great deal of criticism for leaving behind baby Beatrice when she went to Australia soon after the birth, but such an arrangement was once perfectly acceptable.

Prince Charles was never taken on overseas tours, and travel being so much slower in those days, he had longer to miss his parents. He was left behind when his mother went to live in Malta while Prince Philip was posted there. Malta was not considered suitable for a small Royal child.

The new generation of Princes are luckier. The refreshing Princess of Wales has changed everything. In a complete break with protocol, she insisted that she and her husband take Prince William to Australia with them when he was only ten months old, and both Princes joined up with their parents at the end of a State visit to Italy in 1985.

Diana's insistence on not being parted from her children bode badly for Fergie when her turn came. Had Diana not taken William to Australia back in 1983, no doubt everyone would have happily accepted Fergie and Andrew's decision to leave Princess Beatrice behind in 1988.

'Beatrice is much better off at home where things are stable,' Andrew said of his eight-week-old daughter. 'There is no conflict. It would have been possible to bring her but it would have made her life so complicated and disjointed.'

There was one famous photograph taken years ago when Charles' parents were leaving for a tour of Nigeria. It appeared that as they flew off and left him, the small Prince was crying. The nation's heart was wrung by this picture. In fact, the nation's sympathy was misplaced. Charles was not weeping because his beloved parents were flying away. The truth was that he wanted a ride in the airplane and was in a temper because his mother wouldn't take him aboard for a quick trip before she left.

On another occasion when he was seeing off his father on a tour of the Far East, he was pictured with his hand covering his face as if trying to conceal tears. Again public sympathy was misplaced. Charles was, in fact, doing his best to hide the fact that he had lost two front teeth!

Parents are important, of course, but there are many other close and permanent figures in a Royal child's life. Prince Charles had a personal servant from the time he was two years old; a valet called Ian Williams. The Queen and Princess Margaret had their maids, Bobo and Ruby Macdonald. There was little upheaval in the lives of the older generation. Those who cared for them just stayed – not quite as part of the family, but close to it. This new generation is not so lucky. Prince Harry was deeply attached to his first Nanny, Barbara Barnes, who had been at Kensington Palace for five years. It was felt that she was not firm enough with Prince William though in truth one of the problems may have been that she wasn't allowed enough authority. Diana is a doting mother. From the beginning she was determined not to have the kind of old-fashioned nanny who rules absolute and though Prince Charles was disappointed that his old Nanny, Mabel Anderson, was not appointed to bring up his son, he let Diana have her way.

But even modern, non-uniform nannies need support and back-up. And to add to Nanny Barnes' difficulties when William was at his most hectic, his indulgent parents were inclined to laugh. She left by mutual agreement and for days Harry was inconsolable. It is said that when children are sent to boarding school it is Nanny they weep for the first night, and Mummy they weep for the second night. This is almost certainly true of Royal children.

Both William and Harry were upset when their minder, Detective Dave Sharp, was not at Harry's fourth birthday party. Prince Charles felt that the children were becoming too attached to their detective but perhaps this was hardly surprisingly since the detective saw a great deal more of them than their father did. Detective Sharp had been with the little Princes since William was a toddler. But the feeling grew that the bond was becoming too close and it was decided that it would be wiser if Dave Sharp shared his duties with another officer.

Charles and his brothers and sister were also luckier than Harry and Wills in that they had a grandmother who was no longer the Queen and who had all the time in the world for them. The Queen Mother was pretty much an ordinary grandmother, particularly to Charles and Anne while their parents were away. She bathed them and put them to bed and was there to give them a cuddle. They both cut their teeth on an ivory-handled rattle that had once been their mother's and which the Queen Mother had put away for her grandchildren. It then went to Princess Anne's son, Peter, and no doubt will soon be doing valiant duty for Princess Beatrice.

Prince Andrew and Edward had their elder brother about much

of the time. Prince Charles was especially fond of them both and when the Duke was away and the Queen was busy downstairs, he would try to make a point of going in to play with them and read them stories.

Even when he was older, Charles loved the nursery and continued to go there every day for his breakfast, and food was always left on a hot plate for him. To him the nursery represented the home and hearth, particularly in a household where it is difficult to pop in on mummy (as he calls her) because she is either always seeing Very Important People or is out! When the Queen and Prince Philip could join their children, it was for tea – in the nursery. But never unannounced. The staff always knew when either was arriving and much fuss and bother would go on to make sure that everything was in place and that the children were clean and tidy.

In Charles's youth the huge Buckingham Palace nursery was the heart of the building. And while there were moments of panic, in the main everything in the nursery was kept low profile. Nursery staff called the children by their christian names as a hedge again turning small Royals into spoilt brats.

This was at the special order of the Queen who was anxious that the children should be brought up in a no-nonsense manner. She herself practised what she preached. There was a time when she and Princess Anne were riding together and Anne cut her finger on a metal harness when the horse tossed its head.

'Oh!' she said peering closely. 'It's bleeding. It's all red.'

'Not, as you can see, blue!' her mother replied briskly, taking the opportunity to impress once again that she did not want her children growing up believing they were that much different.

Even so, anyone who has worked with Royal children agrees that it is impossible for them not to have an awareness of who they are, and that engenders both respect – and caution.

When their eighteenth birthdays come around the Lord Chamberlain sends out a note to all staff informing them that from that day on the Queen requests that her child be addressed as Your Royal Highness. For those staff who have been very close, it is a difficult switch to make suddenly.

Prince Charles must see a great change in his own children's nursery. Apart from modern nannies about the place, Princess Diana pops in and out of the Highgrove and Kensington Palace nurseries all the time. Her bedroom is within listening distance and the first howl from either child sees her out of bed and in to comfort them. Father did at first try to make her delegate more responsibility to the staff, but her response (not surprisingly from

Diana) was always, 'A mother's arms are more comforting than anyone else's.'

This is something she most certainly feels deeply. In the spring of 1988 Prince Harry had to have an operation on his groin. Happily it wasn't too serious – a small defect which occurs in about one in 250 babies. The little boy went to Great Ormond Street Children's Hospital for the operation. And his mother slept in an adjoining room.

At one time it would have been unthinkable for anyone so close to the Crown to have been allowed anywhere near a hospital. The operation would have taken place at Buckingham Palace. When Princess Margaret had her appendix removed, Great Ormond Street converted her bedroom at Clarence House into a temporary operating theatre, an entire medical team arrived and the offending organ was removed there.

While the Queen was always as healthy as the horses she loves, Princess Margaret's health was never all that good. And young Prince Harry seems to suffer more minor ailments than his big brother. There is even talk of an operation to pin back the stand-out ears – so much the joy of cartoonists – that he has inherited from Prince Charles. George V and George VI were both born with knock-knees; and when Prince Charles was a boy his shoes had to be specially altered to cure the same problem. Like Harry, he was also chesty and prone to coughs and sore throats.

But if Harry does have to go back into hospital at any time, be sure that the Princess of Wales will be there with him.

She undoubtedly feels this way since she lost her own mother at the age of six. She and Fergie have both had to deal with the problem of losing their mothers and being left in the custody of their fathers.

In the Duchess of York's case her father took on the role of both parents to his two daughters quite successfully. He listened to their problems. Sarah's sister, Jane, is two years older than the Duchess, and when their parents broke up she was at that awkward, insecure, anxious age of thirteen. The Major went shopping with the girls, drove them to parties, and above all, showed that he loved them. In Diana's case, her father, who was not a naturally outgoing man, was unable to handle the situation and left the children in the care of servants. Diana wreaked her revenge on a string of nannies and poured all her affection on to her little brother, Charles, whom she mothered as if he were her own.

Most of her considerable warmth and affection is for children whereas one cannot help feeling that most of the Royal Family are basically (in a very British way) more fond of animals. There used to be a sign on the Balmoral estate which read: 'SLOW. Beware Horses, Dogs and Children'. In that order. Princess Diana is not that interested in animals and does not like pets in the house. Nevertheless, William and Harry both have a pony. Harry's is called Smokey and William's, Trigger. There are many horses within the family and there will be other ponies-in-waiting to be brought on as soon as the present ones are outgrown. The boys keep their pet rabbit and their other small pets in the walled garden at Highgrove. They love dogs and William is longing for the day when he can have one of his own. But for the moment he has to make do with his father's Jack Russell, Tigger. During the holidays a special treat is to visit the kennels at Sandringham with their grandmother, the Queen, to see if there are any new puppies. The Queen has always been mad about corgis and even when her children were small there were just as many dogs about the place as there are now. The children were encouraged to play with them and the labradors that are still kept in the kennels of the Great Park at Windsor. The advent of puppies was also a particularly exciting time for Charles and Anne.

The Prince of Wales and his sister grew up loving animals and were encouraged to look after them themselves. There were corgis, caged song-birds called Annie and David in the nursery, and a hamster. In 1954 (when he was six), Charles had a fluffy white rabbit whose name was Harvey – a pet with a couple of rather splendid addresses. Harvey lived in an electrically-heated hutch at Buckingham Palace and when the Court went to Windsor, Harvey went too. Charles refused to be parted from his friend and visited him every morning. He used to clean the rabbit's teeth and cut his toe-nails, as he called them. Old Tom, a veteran member of the Royal mews in those days, had the job of helping the Prince care for his pet. Old Tom kept special brushes, one for Harvey's teeth, one for his fur and another for his claws.

Charles found Harvey a good deal more agreeable than ponies. He was decidedly wary of ponies when young. He liked them well enough as long as he didn't have to get on their backs – and he was always pinching the sugar lumps from the breakfast table to feed them. Some of this earlier dislike of riding may have begun when, after their visit to Britain, the Soviet leaders, Bulganin and Kruschev sent him as a present a Cossack pony named Zamaan. Unfortunately the pony could not walk or trot – it operated only at a fast gallop and Charles hadn't got that far in his riding lessons. As most of the grooms at the stable could testify, Zamaan also had a habit of biting the hand that fed him. Princess Anne would have coped with him, if she hadn't been too small at the time. Later, on holiday in Balmoral, she used to select one of the half-wild hill ponies on the moors and ride it bare-backed wearing a Red Indian head-dress. Needless to say, she did not have her mother's permission for these particular escapades.

Charles was more interested in the pigs at the Home farm which supply the family with pork, ham and bacon. He was always begging Prince Philip to take him to see them. He found them fascinating, particularly when they were being fed – perhaps because they didn't have to watch their table manners in the way that Nanny Lightbody made him watch his. He also learned to snort very realistically.

When it comes to extravagance, the presents that Royal children receive could turn any ordinary child Republican. Prince William has a small replica of an Aston Martin V8 Volante, given to him by the makers. It actually travels at 40 miles an hour and comes in racing green complete with stereo radio and with the same number plates as his father's full-scale Aston Martin. And it cost all of £10,000. In William's nursery there is a rocking horse that was presented by Nancy Reagan. And Princess Beatrice will inherit her father's huge pink rocking elephant which, along with most of the Royal children's toys, is stored at Buckingham Palace waiting for the next generation.

There are quite a lot of those. When he is less destructive, Prince William will probably be given what Prince Charles called the best present he ever had. A gift from the people of Gibraltar, it is a working model of the rock, some 13ft long and 7ft high, 2ft 6in. wide, and a replica in detail down to the last house. There are electrically-operated cranes in the dockyard, model aircraft on the airfield and many of the little houses are lit by electricity. The royal electricians put it together while the family were at Balmoral as a surprise for when Charles returned home to Buckingham Palace.

From Gibraltar with love to Anne there was an all-electric doll's bungalow, so big at 7ft long, 4ft high and 2ft deep that the Princess could crawl into it. Charles also had a three-masted schooner almost big enough for him to go aboard, and it was kept in the dry dock in the Mariner's Hut in the Palace gardens.

The Little House (Y Bwthyn Bach) a gift from the people of Wales to Princess Elizabeth and her sister is still at Royal Lodge at Windsor. It was their favourite toy, with windows that open, plumbing, a radio that works, and lights that switch on and off. Even a make-believe insurance policy was kept in a drawer of the oak dresser. An adult can only get in on hands and knees, but there is one point on the landing where it is possible for a small grown woman to stand upright.

When Elizabeth and Margaret returned to London they wrapped the Little House's silver in newspaper to 'stop it getting tarnished', put away the linen and covered the furniture with dust sheets, just like the staff did in their own home.

This toy never featured in arguments when the Queen and her sister were small. The house was passed on down to Charles and Anne less peacefully. Anne used to lock herself in when they quarrelled, leaving an angry Charles outside trying to kick the door down.

There is also a 6ft 9in. miniature caravan that was given to Charles and Anne as children. They held their tea parties inside where no adult could enter. It has now been passed on to Diana's children.

But all this excess does not seem to have spoilt Harry. In 1988 he was taken to see Father Christmas at Harrods and Father Christmas asked what present he really wanted. 'A slice of Christmas cake,' replied Harry cheerfully and endearingly.

And Fergie has given Beatrice her favourite toy from childhood – a battered, life-size bunny. Perhaps the intention is that it should be company for the pile of teddy bears that decorate Bea's nursery.

Royal children love their teddies and it was a true act of kindness when Prince Philip, Princess Margaret, the Princess Royal, the Duke and Duchess of Kent and Princess Alexandra all loaned their teddies to the Great Ormond Street Teddy Bear Museum to help raise funds.

It seems that the Prince of Wales was not prepared even temporarily to part with his. Prince Charles is superstitious about his teddy, and even when he was a grown man it used to travel with him. He once left it behind when he was on an overseas tour.

It was sent on to him aboard the next jet.

# Upstairs Downstairs And Somewhere In Between

With the dawn of the twenty-first century almost within grasp, Pages of the Back Stairs and Pages of the Presence could surely only be part of the cast of Cinderella or some Ruritanian-style opera. In fact, bearers of these archaic titles are alive and well, and working in Buckingham Palace.

The Queen and Prince Philip each have two Pages of the Back Stairs. These four men probably see more of the Queen and her husband than any member of the Royal Family. At least two of the four are always on call. The Queen's Page of the Back Stairs stands behind her chair when she dines, and Her Majesty finds him a source of much Palace gossip when she is relaxing in her own apartments.

In times gone by, the task of the Pages of the Back Stairs was to take the King's mistress or the Queen's lover up via the backstairs to the Royal bed chamber. Not unnaturally they were chosen for their complete trustworthiness. They are chosen for the same reasons of trustworthiness today but happily their role has changed.

The title 'Page' causes some confusion with foreign visitors. When the Reagans stayed at Windsor, the Queen lent the President one of her Pages, and Prince Philip lent Nancy one of his. Their most important task on this occasion was to liaise with the President's staff to make sure that nothing went wrong with any of the arrangements, particularly the timing. Nobody fancied finding the Queen tapping her foot and twisting her engagement

41

ring around her finger (a sign of annoyance) while she waited for the Reagans to keep an appointment.

Behind the green baize door at Windsor the American Secret Service men were highly amused when they saw these fellows in their black tailcoats and beige knee-breeches running around after the President and his wife. They were not quite what they had anticipated. The bemused visitors had been expecting small boys.

People always expect Pages to be young boys. One of the Queen's Pages, now retired, tells of the time he went to Nigeria with the Queen. He was on the accommodation list as E. Bennett, Queen's Page. When he arrived in his room, he found it was full of toys and furnished with a tiny cot. The Nigerians were astonished when E. Bennett, Page, turned out to be a man in his forties.

Some of the Queen's Pages are, in fact, boys. But these are the four Pages of Honour, the sons of nobility whose job in the Royal pageant is to carry the Queen's train at the State Opening of Parliament or on any other occasion when she wears robes. It is hardly a job for life. They retire at sixteen.

The Pages of the Back Stairs and the Pages of the Presence are high on the pecking order of the 160 Staff it takes to keep Buckingham Palace ticking over.

The Queen's Staff maintain their own strict order of precedence which they guard jealously. Most of them wear some kind of uniform or livery, and twenty-four hold senior positions. Staff are split into two sections. There are those who work in the Palace and those who work in the Royal mews – the grooms, the postillions, the ten chauffeurs, carriage drivers, etc. This second group are mostly horsey people and usually recruited from the Life Guards and other mounted regiments. There are no female grooms in London, though a few are hired to look after the polo ponies at Windsor. The mews are under the control of the Crown Equerry, who is not classed as staff, but as a member of the Queen's Household. The Household is the smarter members of those who serve the Royal Family – mostly garnered from the aristocracy. When members of the Queen's Household leave one of her Palaces and Castles they usually go home to a palace or castle of their own or at very least a grace and favour house on one of the Queen's estates.

The Royal Mews also houses the few married men who work for the Queen, and there are several grand houses backing onto the Mews in Lower Grosvenor Gardens. One of these is traditionally occupied by the King's valets and next door is allocated to the Superintendent of the Royal Mews – the number two to the Crown Equerry.

Oddly it is the ordinary members of staff who are often closest to the Royals and who, away from the spotlight, get to know them best. It is these members of staff who can tell immediately what sort of mood their employers are in. They know what irritates and what pleases because their most senior members have often been in the Queen's service since an early age. Cyril Dickman, the Palace Steward, is the number one in the staff hierachy – he started life at the Palace as a footman and worked his way up. He is assisted by a Deputy Palace Steward who is also called the Groom of the Chambers – another of those archaic titles. The Deputy shares equal rank with the Royal valets and dressers, and then next in importance come the anachronistic Pages of the Back Stairs.

Even though they belong to the Queen's Staff, the Pages of the Back Stairs have considerable power in the Palace. Palace Officials, including the Private Secretaries, have to petition through these Pages before they can gain access to either the Queen or Prince Philip. Officials are the middle levels of Royal employees, the nine-to-five workers, accountants, secretaries and clerks who regard Buckingham Palace as the office. Jealousy can creep in, in the relationship between staff and officials, possibly because the officials rarely set eyes on a member of the Royal Family and staff see them all the time. And the staff don't care for what they regard as the officials' superior attitudes.

When the officials are dealing with the Pages they have been known to become paranoid, imagining that the Pages are blocking their way. Indeed, sometimes this does happen, but at Royalty's behest. The system of using a Page as an intermediary suits the Royal Family. They leave their Pages to tell the white lies, make the excuses or inform people that Her Majesty is otherwise engaged when the truth is that Her Majesty doesn't wish to get involved just at the moment. Like us, the Royal Family occasionally puts things off.

It is heady power for the Pages, but other than the close contact they enjoy with their famous employers, they are little more than glorified butlers.

The Queen Mother has Pages. Prince Charles and the Princess of Wales do not. Pages and Majesty go together. The Waleses are not yet high enough on the ladder. The top staff rank in the Waleses household is butler, followed by footman. The Monarch is never upstaged, not even by the heir and certainly not by anyone else. Years ago the Queen's father, King George VI, heard that the Lord Mayor of London had appointed unto himself a Sergeant Footman.

'There is only one Sergeant Footman in England,' roared the King, 'and he is mine.'

Next in the staff pecking order come the Queen's four yeomen. These are nothing to do with those at the Tower of London who are basically sentries. The Queen's Yeoman are senior domestic staff.

The Yeoman of the Plate looks after all the Queen's gold and silver plate and cutlery – the finest in the world. He has six helpers, all of whom are called under-butlers and they care for what is an amazing treasure-trove. After every use, the hundreds of plates, candlesticks, and table-centres are carefully counted, washed in hot soapy water, wrapped in airtight bags and stored in a specially-made locked vault in the basement. Yes, spoons sometimes do go missing!

There was a time when many other things went missing. The mad Duke of Connaught melted a lot of it down. At a garden party in King George V's reign, a large contingent of American guests managed to remove, as souvenirs, more than a thousand pieces of silver, mostly cake forks and tea spoons. Since then the Royals have hired the cutlery for the Royal Garden Parties from Joe Lyons, the caterers. For many years all the gold and silver was kept in an Aladdin's cave of a storeroom just fifty yards from the Trade Gate of the Palace. All that was needed to get inside was one big key. A new Master of the Household, Hardy Roberts, had a fit when he saw how simple it would be to steal this amazing collection of gold and silver plates, huge candelabras, cruet sets and serving dishes along with a mixed bag of family heirlooms.

It was he who had the gold and silver moved to a basement vault which was once an air-raid shelter and an alarm, wired to the Palace police station, was installed. But even so, it was only a few years ago that a solid silver tea service completely disappeared.

The Yeoman of the Glass and China oversees the setting of the tables for any grand or State occasion. He has four assistants and they look after the Queen's incredible collection of crystal and china. The Yeoman of the Glass and China knows exactly where to put his hands on any one of the hundreds of glasses and dozens of bone china services which are scattered in cabinets around the Palace. These, too, are all carefully washed and dried by hand. Dishwashers would do nothing to improve the delicate gold decorations.

The staff who look after these beautiful things become very possessive of them, treating them as if they were their own.

The Yeoman of the Wine Cellars and his two helpers have their territory in the basement where all the Palace wines and spirits are kept at a carefully controlled temperature. It is their responsibility to order the thousands of bottles of wine, spirits and soft drinks for the hundreds of guests who come to the Palace.

The Travelling Yeoman is the newest of these appointments. His job is to take care of all the Queen's travel arrangements, both in England and abroad. He is also responsible for moving the Queen's large staff around the different Royal residences. He does this with the help of the Army who move the Royal Family's considerable luggage everytime they move house.

When the Queen goes on a State visit abroad, if she is staying at the British Embassy and giving a banquet for the host country, she will often take all four of her yeomen with her. She also takes her own gold plate, her own china and crystal and her own wines. The Embassy, for the night, could easily be a miniature Buckingham Palace.

Next in pecking order of importance, after the yeomen, come the four Pages of the Presence. These men look after the Queen's Household and act as ushers and guides at formal State occasions. They are much in demand at Windsor Castle which is so big that everyone gets lost.

One step down from the ordinary Pages are the footmen. The most senior is the Sergeant Footman, who, as George VI emphasized belongs to the Monarch and no one else. The Sergeant Footman answers only to the Queen herself. At one time he used to make all the travel arrangements for the Monarch, but this became too large a task – and the Travelling Yeoman has taken over this aspect of the job. The Sergeant Footman has a deputy and a dozen or so other footmen beneath him and who are on duty in the Palace at any time. They serve at table, act as valet for any guest who hasn't one of his own, take the Queen's corgis for a walk, run messages and ride attendant on the back of the Royal coaches.

Then comes the Nursery Footman who's main function is to run around after Nanny. But since the only royal baby at the moment is Princess Beatrice and she is not in permanent residence in the Palace, the role has almost become extinct. In fact, the nursery quarters were turned into an apartment for Prince Andrew after Charles married and left home. Again, Charles and Diana are not yet grand enough to have a nursery footman – they 'make do' with nursery maids.

The footmen can be an irreverent lot. On days when their Mistress and Master are a touch scratchy, behind their backs they call the Queen and Prince Philip 'Mother and Father'. And one who once worked for Princess Anne referred to her as Anne

Elizabeth Alice Louise (her full name) whenever she was in a bad temper.

On the other hand, Royalty call their policemen and chauffeurs by their surnames, (though the less formal Princess Diana is inclined to give them nicknames), footmen and valets by their christian names, their Pages and older staff by their surnames.

Valets and dressers consider that they have the best of the staff jobs and are fortunate to have such close contact with Royalty. Their duties are mainly concerned with dress but valets have an extra task. They are sent to Purdey's or Holland and Holland, the gunsmiths, where they are given brief lessons in handling a gun. Once they are sufficiently skilled to be safe with a firearm in their hands, they act as loaders for their masters on shooting weekends.

One of Prince Philip's valets, Joe Pearce, died in harness when the Queen and Prince Philip were guests at a shooting party at Lord Dalhousie's estate in Scotland. It happened when the Duke was out in front with Joe a pace away loading for him. The Queen was well behind, working the dogs and picking up the dead grouse. Suddenly ahead of her she saw one of the two figures fall. For one awful moment she thought it was the Duke and ran as fast as she could to where the men were.

It was Joe Pearce who had dropped dead from a heart attack and both the Duke and the Queen were deeply saddened by his death. The valet had been the Queen's personal footman while she was still Princess Elizabeth and living at Clarence House. She had known him a very long time and he was part of the family. A memorial service was arranged for him in St James Church, Piccadilly, which the Duke attended.

There are few women employed in Staff, but the Queen's House-keeper, Miss Colebrook, is probably one of the most powerful people in the Palace. She controls all the women staff, including four other housekeepers for Balmoral, Windsor, Sandringham and Holyrood House in Edinburgh; she hires the daily helps who keep the Queen's vast homes impeccably clean; she chooses rooms for guests and checks that all is well before the Queen herself personally escorts her visitors to their rooms. In the past Miss Colebrook would have been known as Mrs Colebrook, a 'courtesy' title that once was given to all Royal housekeepers regardless of whether they were married or not. The Palace has come into the twentieth century since the appointment of Miss Colebrook, but her christian name is still not used.

There are about twenty-four housemaids employed in the Pal-ace. These are kept well segregated from the male staff. They are quartered in the right-hand corner of the Palace while the men are all on the left. The reverse applies to the Royal Family themselves. The male apartments are traditionally to the right of the inner quadrangle and the entrance to the Palace, called the King's Door, is on the right. The only time the Queen ever uses this door is when she leaves for Trooping the Colour.

These housemaids who do the basic housework with help from dailies are not supposed to be seen or heard. Their work is usually done while no one is about. If they do unexpectedly hear a member of the Royal Family coming, they will go to extraordinary lengths to keep out of the way. The Queen's Uncle, the late Duke of Gloucester, had a housemaid called Annie who was dismayed to hear her master coming down the stairs just as she was sweeping them. She shot into the nearest broom cupboard, pulling the door shut behind her.

The door promptly re-opened and Gloucester stuck his head round it. 'Morning, Annie,' he said, and shut the door on her again.

There was a similar incident involving Queen Mary. The difference was that she opened the cupboard door and said, 'Please don't hide, my dear. I do so like to see people around the place.'

In the normal way, the working women don't get to see a member of the family very often but on Jubilee Day in 1977 they were given a treat. The entire staff, including housemaids, were allowed to line the corridors to the Grand Entrance when the Queen was leaving Buckingham Palace for the St Paul's Service of Thanksgiving. As she came into the well-like entrance, the entire staff burst into cheers.

She stood stock still for a moment, looking as if she might cry. But the Monarch never shows any emotion. She recovered, smiled, waved and walked to her carriage, the baubles on her pink hat swinging jauntily. No one who was fortunate enough to be there will ever forget that most moving moment.

Apart from cleaning and dusting, housemaids are meant to deliver breakfast to the ladies – the footmen are not allowed into bedrooms if a woman is sleeping there.

This is not always possible. Some of the silver breakfast trays, once loaded, are far too heavy for a woman to carry. The compromise is that a housemaid hovers in the doorway while a footman carries in the tray.

The Palace does not employ married woman even if they marry a fellow employee. The Queen often recruits her staff in Scotland

and many years ago three sisters called Hamilton who lived near Balmoral went to work at the Palace.

One married the Palace Steward, the second married the Deputy Page of Chambers, and the third married one of the Palace chefs. And all three girls had to leave.

But while employed, women staff do have one special privilege which they very much enjoy. On glittering State occasions the housemaids are allowed to line the corridors and watch Her Majesty and the guests of honour go into dinner. At least it means that they have been within touching distance of some of the most famous and important people in the world. With all the maids curtseying as the Queen goes by it is extremely grand and impressive for the visitors, too.

Women members of the staff are also allowed to use the Palace gardens, providing no member of the Royal Family is there. The rules have now been relaxed so that if the tennis courts are free, the staff may use them too. But as a rule the only staff seen regularly in the gardens are footmen walking the Queen's dogs. Again, only if the Queen herself is not about.

A story which particularly illustrates this rule concerns one of Prince Charles' valets. Prince Charles owned a fine labrador called Harvey (named, one supposes, after his childhood pet rabbit), whom the Queen herself had bred for her son at the Sandringham kennels. One afternoon Prince Charles asked the valet if he would give Harvey a run around the gardens. The valet checked with the Queen's Page that Her Majesty was safe in her own rooms. On being assured that she was, he took the dog out into the grounds.

He had been walking for only five minutes or so when he saw a familar figure in a head-scarf, corgis at heel, walking briskly towards him. He rapidly set off in another direction, hoping that the Queen hadn't spotted him. But in the whole forty acres of the Palace Garden he seemed unable to shake her off. Whichever way he turned, she suddenly appeared again.

Eventually the corgis came bounding towards Harvey and the valet was face to face with the Queen. 'I did ask the Page', he said, and started to apologise.

'No, no, no,' she said. 'I've been trying to catch you up. I saw you walking Harvey from my window and I wanted to see how he is. I didn't know he was in London.'

Explanations over, the valet was not surprised at her interest. The Queen rarely loses track of any of the dogs she breeds and always likes to know if they are well and happy. But it was a pretty ludicrous situation – the Queen rushing about her own garden, trying to catch her son's valet who was equally intent on avoiding her.

Buckingham Palace and the other Royal homes are living remnants of the old upstairs downstairs system which barely survives anymore. Unlike the old days, no one who works for the Queen is exploited. When it comes to the personal servants whom the family see every day there is a closeness. Often the staff get away with murder, but the Queen likes to let it be known that she is aware of this.

Cheese savoury is as popular below stairs as above and the Queen noticed that when this was on the menu the chef always provided portions much larger than she and her husband could possibly eat. After being served with the savoury one day, before the footman was out of the door, she said in a loud, clear voice that he couldn't possibly miss, 'Please don't eat too much, Philip. We must leave some for the staff because they like it so much.'

Her reproofs are gentle. After lunch one day the footman found a slug from her salad carefully placed on a piece of paper. With it was a note which read, 'Could you eat this?'

The note would have been written in pencil. Royalty use pencils for all memos, and they write everything down. Princess Margaret has a thing about people pinching her pencils. She is always ringing down for a new one. 'Take my gold, take my Fabergé,' she will sigh, 'but please leave me my pencils!'

They are great believers in little notes – that way there cannot be any mistakes. For example, when the Queen plans to go riding the next morning she leaves her Page a memo naming particular horses to get ready, and it is his job to convey the information to the grooms.

Those who work for Royalty do not earn a fortune. Although there is now a small union branch at the Palace, they don't find much to complain about. Everything is 'all in' so that salary is basically pocket money. The Queen is a considerate employer. There is a first-class canteen for the staff which is more like a club, and the drinks are all served at cost. The staff bedrooms have the best view in London and it is, after all, a very good address.

If staff retire in the Queen's service they can expect a small pension and a grace and favour home to live in, probably somewhere on either the Windsor and Sandringham Estates or the Duchy of Cornwall property around Kennington in South London. It is not so long since Prince Philip had a row of houses built on the Windsor Estate since they were running short of accomodation for retired staff.

They do often go on working. When the Palace is short of help they are called back temporarily at very advantageous rates. The Queen's retainers can rely on being safely protected for the rest of their lives.

Those who live in the Palace all have good-sized rooms of their own, pleasantly furnished and with a kitchen nearby which three or four members of staff can share. Not everyone goes to Windsor at the weekend with the Queen, and when she is not in the Palace the main kitchens shut down. Those who stay therefore have to fend for themselves, so the Palace is dotted with small kitchens. Rooms for longer-serving staff are always identifiable by the china cabinet in pride of place. It will be filled with the china that the Queen has given them as Christmas presents over the years. Prince Charles' staff at Highgrove have a very charming sitting-room that is furnished with the contents of Princess Diana's Colehearne Court flat – where she lived before she married. There are pretty floral curtains, wicker furniture and sofas with the cushions she is so fond of.

And, naturally, there are perks. Some Royal staff do a bit of moonlighting in their free time. Other members of the Royal Family will occasionally take on some of the Queen's staff if they are giving a party or need more help. They don't have to ask the Queen. They just ring the Palace Steward and ask if he can spare a couple of footmen or cooks. The Duke and Duchess of Kent and Princess Michael of Kent frequently hire Palace staff for the evening. So do foreign embassies, grand receptions at London's livery halls, and even at smart private homes the waiters often include some of the Queen's footmen. Her chefs moonlight, too. It brings in extra money. The Queen once went to a Livery Company dinner to find that her Chef was cooking it. She didn't mind. It is an accepted practice. And at least at outside parties where Royal staff are in attendance anyone from the Palace knows that their glass will always be kept well-filled and they will be well attended to.

Those members of staff who go on overseas tours with the family often receive presents from the host country. The Household group may be given a watch or piece of jewellery of some kind. The staff can, also, anticipate a really good tip, though it may turn out to be a present. The same happens when distinguished visitors come to Britain as the Queen's guests. Those from the East are favourites; for example, the late Shah of Persia's aides who tipped with gold coins.

When the Queen went to Saudi Arabia in 1979, her tour coincided with a Customs strike. One evening at dinner during the visit she said to the Duke: 'I've just been on the phone to Mother who tells me that the Customs strike is still on at home. Good news for some, I thought, with all their lovely presents.'

The Page behind her chair could hardly keep a straight face.

However, any member of the Queen's staff who was deliberately involved with smuggling would certainly lose his or her job. The only reasons for sackings at the Palace are dishonesty, immorality or actions that reflect against the dignity of the Crown.

When someone does have to be dismissed, the Queen will put on her wellington boots and go for a long walk with the corgis until it is all over. Having to let a member of her staff go upsets her and as she always worries that they might make a direct appeal to her, she thinks it best to keep out of the way.

Like any other employer, it is not easy for the Queen to sack unsatisfactory staff. The Master of the Household has to give the offender three warnings. Staff can only be instantly dismissed if they do something that the Queen, as the Monarch, cannot, in her position, condone.

One of her footmen was dismissed for chasing a young sailor around the dining-room on the Royal Yacht.

As she is head of the Church of England a sexual offence is a firing matter and as she is head of the bench and the law is her law, breaking it is therefore a firing matter too.

Two footmen bit the dust when it was discovered that, having a passion for explosives, they had been robbing mines around the country for sticks of gelignite, using a stolen car. Incredibly, one of them had asked at a Buckingham Palace staff welfare meeting if he could keep a lathe in his room. This request was greeted with some surprise since some of the footmen are said to be more into embroidery than metalwork! The Master, perhaps thinking that at least the macho Prince Philip would approve, gave his permission.

The footman used the lathe to make false number-plates for the stolen Landrover which he had the cool nerve to park in the Palace forecourt.

When the stolen explosives were discovered in the Palace, panic set in. There was a real fear that the footmen might have been IRA infiltrators. But no, the problem was merely an excessive interest in explosives. Nevertheless, both men went to jail.

Two more went on their way rapidly when they were heard on a Kent train chattering indiscreetly about their jobs. Nor were they being particularly flattering about their employers. They both came from the college of catering in Thanet where the Palace recruit staff.

They had the misfortune to be overheard by 'Outraged of Tunbridge Wells', who felt it her duty to write to the Palace, saying that if these two young men were typical examples of Royal staff, then she had great sympathy for the Queen.

It wasn't difficult to identify them, and they were informed that their services were no longer required.

There is a considerable turn-over of staff at the Palace. People take a job there out of curiosity. Some find the money is not good enough or realise that domestic service is still domestic service, even in a Palace. But many stay all their working lives.

Princess Anne and Princess Michael have the highest turnover in staff. Princess Anne has little in the way of permanent staff. Gatcombe Park is kept clean by daily women. Staff of the old school dislike working there because they don't feel that things are 'done in the right way'. In Princess Michael's case the problem is that because the Michaels are hard up, the staff are expected to be head cooks and bottle washers. The butler doubles as the chauffeur, and sometimes as general handy-man. And they often don't like it. When the Princess bought Nether Lypiatt, her house in Gloucestershire, she took a butler down one weekend to unpack and sort things out.

She suddenly said to him, 'Do you like painting?' Thinking she meant painting in oils or water-colours. He thought about it for a moment and then said, 'I'd like to try, but I don't know if I'd be any good at it.'

'In that case,' she replied, 'perhaps you could have a go at painting the stables next week.' He painted the stables, but he handed in his notice soon afterwards.

It must be said that the Royal Family do manage to live a relaxed and comparatively lazy life, doing little for themselves. The late Duke of Gloucester was once snoozing by an open fire at his home, Barnwell Manor, when a log fell onto the carpet. The Duke did nothing. Fortunately a footman was passing the door and smelt smoke. He rushed in picked up the log and stamped out the burning mat. The Duke was heard to grunt, 'About time too.'

Those members of staff who serve the Royals so closely are often treated with considerable affection. In no way would they consider themselves 'friends' of the family, but they are certainly part of the family and everyone, staff and Royal, are aware of their place in hierarchy.

Royalty rarely visit the basement of the Palace where the kitchens are situated. Prince Philip has been known to storm down if the food isn't to his liking. Prince Charles meant to visit to say thank you to the staff after the pre-wedding party he gave for 400 guests but had forgotten the way and never got there.

The Queen once made a surprise call to thank the Chef for a particularly delicious meal. The duty chef, who was thrilled by her unexpected appearance, had been working for her for more than seventeen years.

On her way back to her own rooms, she passed one of her Yeomen. 'What is the name of that chef who is on duty today?' she asked him. The Yeoman told her, and then full of glee and mischief, raced back down to the kitchen.

'Oh, it *was* you,' he said, all sweetness and light. 'The Queen couldn't remember you at all.'

The chef was both hurt and furious and went around banging pots and muttering, 'seventeen years'. He was a victim of the intense rivalry between the staff who all like to imagine that they are closer and better known to the Royals than the next man.

But all ended well. Not long afterwards a good position came up with the Queen Mother. The slighted chef applied, landed the job and stayed.

The Queen Mother's staff do stay with her, and perhaps one of the secrets of her success is that she never gives anyone a direct order. For example, she loathes cooking smells in the house, and should the faintest drift of bacon and eggs come floating through she will say quietly to a Page, 'Do you think someone could do something about that?'

In turn her loyal staff will do anything for her. Like the rest of the Royals, she is very much an outdoor person, and she likes best to lunch in the garden at Clarence House, sitting under the trees. Not surprisingly, the English climate makes this something of a problem. The staff have to keep a weather eye out. Sometimes they will be running in and out all morning, setting up tables and then if the sky darkens, taking them back in again.

But the staff can be touchy, too. At the beginning of 1989, Julian Loyd (old Etonian father of Alexandra, one of Princess Diana's ladies-in-waiting), who runs Sandringham Estate, put a protocol guide into the pay-packets of the 130 staff.

It stated tersely that the Queen must first be addressed as 'Your Majesty' and then afterwards as 'Ma'am'. Men must take off their hats when meeting her, and all the Princesses should be called 'Your Royal Highness', and then 'Ma'am'. All Princes should be greeted as Your Royal Highness and thereafter as 'Sir'.

The older Staff were deeply offended that anyone should think they needed to be told something they had known for all their years of Royal service, but apparently the instructions came about when one young gamekeeper upset Princess Anne by saying a cheerful 'cheerio' to her.

One can hardly blame him. Princess Anne is the least formal of all the Royals and her switches from simplicity to grandeur can be confusing. She is too much her mother's daughter to accept familiarity, but she still tries to live as normally as possible. So much so that when she hired a temporary butler and he turned up faultlessly dressed for the job in pin-striped trousers and black jacket, she looked at him doubtfully and said, 'Haven't you got anything a bit less formal? Our butler usually wears jeans.'

Princess Margaret can cause the same kind of problems. It is said that she never seems to know from one day to the next whether she wants to be treated as the Little Princess, Cinderella or a combination of both.

She employed one butler who put up with a great deal. It was in the days when her health was better and she was forever out at nightclubs and came home well after midnight. She often appeared with a party of people, and expected supper for all.

At some ungodly hour the harassed butler would be trying to rustle something up from the refrigerator knowing that he would get hell from the chef the next morning.

One day, exasperated by something the Princess had done, the butler announced that he was leaving and this time he meant it. 'Well,' said the Princess, her huge blue eyes beguiling, 'if you are going, I'm going too.'

He stayed.

The Prince and Princess of Wales have also had more than their fair share of staff problems over the last seven years. Wages could be better, standards are high and hours are long. But the rapid turnover so apparent when Diana first arrived on the scene has recently slowed down. They have had their present butler, Harold Brown, since 1984 when Alan Fisher left. Alan Fisher spent less than three years with the Waleses, and reputedly left because he was bored. A highly experienced butler, having been with both the Duke and Duchess of Windsor and Bing Crosby for many years, he might well have found working for Prince Charles a little on the quiet side. In the early days of their marriage, Charles and Diana hardly entertained at all, and the professional Fisher found himself answering the telephone, posting letters and doing little in the way of real butlering. It was exasperating for someone so skilled. Indeed, he once said rather crossly to Prince Charles that if they ever did get around to giving a dinner party, say for twenty-four, he would be happy to organise things for them.

Charles and Diana had found him when he had been working on a casual basis for Diana's father, the Earl of Spencer, and were highly impressed. When they approached him to see if he would be interested in a full-time job with them, they were surprised to find that he had already approached Prince Charles' household on two occasions and been turned down. He was promptly taken on at Kensington Palace and Prince Charles asked some awkward questions in his office.

Though Fisher left, he holds the Princess in great esteem and will not hear a word said against her.

'All I will say,' he says, 'is that it should be the privilege of everyone, once in their lifetime, to work for someone like the Princess of Wales. I say this, having looked into those sapphire blue eyes – from three feet – for over two and a half years.'

Fisher's successor, Harold Brown, is an unassuming, quiet man whose hobby is collecting royal archive photographs, which he has been doing for many years. He used to work for Prince and Princess Michael of Kent where he was very popular but not always up to her demanding standards. She trained him very carefully only to find that he had been approached by the neighbours – the Waleses, who poached him. She was not unduly upset as she appreciated his ambition to work for the future King.

Brown is very happy with his present employers, but was somewhat embarrassed when a couple of years ago the *Daily Mirror* set him up and 'exposed' him for moonlighting. Brown can be hired to serve at cocktail parties and the newspaper, under a false name, booked him. They photographed him and ran the story under a 'Royal Butler for Sale' type headline. What the newspaper did not mention was that moonlighting is accepted in Palace life.

Detectives, chefs and housemaids, all have a fairly fast turnover because the hours are so unsocial and the quarters overcrowded. But since early in 1988 all Prince Charles' office staff have been moved to St James' Palace where they occupy the Lord Chamberlain's old set of rooms. Charles also has an office there overlooking a public road next to the Chapel Royal. His insistence on throwing the windows wide open has given the security men a headache. They feel that he could be a target for a sniper's bullet and have advised the Prince to move his rooms further to the back of the building if he must have the windows open.

Nannies rank high in the Palace heirarchy. They get their own flat and their own footman and are held in higher esteem than almost any other employee. The Queen's children were all brought up by Nanny Mabel Anderson and she is the only person outside the family who calls them all by their christian names. Even Lady Diana called Prince Charles 'Sir' in public until they were engaged, though she spent a lot of time trying to avoid calling him anything. Nanny Anderson, a Scottish policeman's daughter, is the only person outside the family who still gives the Royal Princes a kiss. She was also the only person in the Palace who could pop in on the Prince of Wales for a chat anytime she liked. This would sometimes enrage Squadron Leader David Checketts, who was the Prince's private secretary. If he couldn't get in to see the Prince because Nanny was ensconced for a cosy chat, Checketts would bang about and mutter that his life was constantly being thwarted by nannies!

When Nanny Anderson was away, a plump, jolly lady called Nanny Bunn used to take care of Prince Edward and Prince Andrew. She was the perfect traditional nanny. What puzzled the Queen's staff was that Prince Philip, who never so much as spoke to Nanny Anderson if he could avoid it, appeared quite fond of Nanny Bunn. He would ask her and the children to join him for lunch if he were eating alone. None of the staff ever worked out why. Another much-loved Nanny was the aptly named Nanny Rattle who brought up Princess Alexandra's children.

Sadly, Mabel Anderson is no longer with the Royal Family. Prince Charles was most anxious that she was nanny to his children, but Diana had other ideas.

For a while Mabel did go to Gatcombe Park to look after Peter and Zara Philips for Princess Anne but it didn't work out. Gatcombe Park was run so casually that Nanny had to take her own food up to the nursery, clean it and do everything for the children. After so many years in the Buckingham Palace nursery where there were always two footmen and nursery maids to do her bidding, she found it hard to adjust. Eventually she went off to another appointment where 'things were done properly'.

Princess Diana's present Nanny, Ruth Wallace, has not had any formal training (she was a nurse), but worked for Princess Michael of Kent who prides herself on training excellent staff. For six years Ruth Wallace looked after Freddie and Ella Windsor, the Kents' children, and their manners were the envy of all their Royal aunts and uncles.

'Your Nanny must be good,' Prince Charles said to Princess Michael. 'Your children have the most beautiful manners.'

He thought Ruth Wallace was so good he had no compuction about encouraging Diana to poach her – just as they had the butler. Once again Princess Michael swallowed her pride. Ruth Wallace was getting more money and more glory and, as Princess Michael says, 'The Princess of Wales is a lovely person. How could I be cross with her?'

The curious thing about the women who work for Royal women is that they seldom seem to get on with the man of the house. It comes, of course, from an understandable and terrific loyalty to their mistresses. They appear to devote their lives to the Royal mistress to the extent of handwashing their underwear and hand-kerchiefs. They never marry. And in the world of nannies, men often seem to be the enemy.

Princess Margaret employed a wonderful woman called Nanny Sumner to look after her two children. Nanny Sumner was both a pillar of strength and much loved by all. She brought up Sarah Armstrong-Jones and Lord Linley beautifully; she made them share things and mind their manners. They have both turned out to be charming adults. But Nanny Sumner could not be doing with Lord Snowdon, and the feeling appeared to be mutual – a shame, since they are both such nice people. Other women employed by Princess Margaret – her dresser and her house manager – both felt the same way. There were no tears from any of them when Lord Snowdon left. The concensus of opinion was that everything could get back to normal now they had the Princess to themselves again.

The same situation existed at Princess Alexandra's home, where apparently her personal maid was not too enamoured with Angus Ogilvy. And Bobo Macdonald, the Queen's maid and dresser, has never really approved of Prince Philip. It is said that she did not feel that he was anywhere near good enough for her Little Lady.

But the remarkable Bobo is another story and deserving of a chapter all to herself . . . .

She is positive proof that something very akin to friendship can come between servant and master, even in Royal situations. It happens between nannies, dressers, valets and their Royal charges. Policemen can become almost indispensible, too. The Royal Family are not remotely snobbish. In fact their personal complaint about the British aristocracy generally is that they are the most colossal snobs and 'much too grand for us'.

In his bachelor days Prince Charles had his own three musket-eers. Two policemen, Paul Officer and John McClean, and his valet, Stephen Barry. This trio enjoyed a true companionship with their boss, though none would presume to say that the Prince was their friend.

It is not really surprising that the Prince took so long to marry. As a single man he could go shooting, fishing, flying, sailing, riding, – do anything he wanted – with a trusted policeman and valet who were exactly his age for companionship. There were few restrictions and plenty of girlfriends.

Charles and his musketeers shared many adventures together. McClean, Barry and the Prince, along with Nicholas Soames who was acting as Equerry, all stayed together at Funafuti on the Gilbert and Ellice Islands when the Prince went there to deliver a message from the Queen in the late 1970s.

They stayed in a large hut just off the beach, divided by screens, which John McClean christened the Funafuti Hilton. It was not unlike a hospital ward, and the Prince was given the most privacy. He had two screens. They all slept, ignoring each other's snores, in this close proximity. They were young and they had fun.

Stephen Barry also recalled a few days that were spent in Venezuela:

'Four of us, the Prince, Squadron Leader Checketts, John McClean and I, all flew to a dusty airstrip right up in the mountains to a place called Lake Caribou. It was the spot that had given Jules Verne the inspiration for *The Lost World*. We saw his point. All there was when we landed were three or four huts and a few staff to look after us.

'Their first duty was to paddle the four of us in a canoe, with all our luggage, further along the river to a camp site. Right bang in the middle of nowhere it consisted of two sheds, two huts and a barbecue hut.

'The Venezuelan Government flew in very good food and we were just left to our own devices for two days. It was primitive but comfortable . . . .

'The silence was the most extraordinary thing. We were so high in the mountains that the only sound was made by the river as it rushed by – far too broad and rapid, alas, for swimming.

'The heat made everything shimmer and we just lazed about, eating and sleeping and getting very tanned. The place was so remote that in the cool of the night one felt a little uneasy, wondering how anyone could survive there. But we were surviving with delicious food, plenty to drink, and enjoying much the same kind of barbecue that the Prince likes in the Highlands of Scotland.

"Supposing someone came round that bend in the river and saw us all sitting here, eating," the Prince said. "Wouldn't they get a surprise."

"They would if they realised who you are, sir," I said.

'The Prince slept in a hut by himself, in a single bunk. In the shed next door the policeman bedded down, while Squadron Leader Checketts and I shared the other hut with two bunks. It was a strange experience.'

And it was one of many that could not fail to cement special relationships between Royal servant and master. But they were to end when the Prince married. Paul Officer left on the wedding day; John McClean and Stephen Barry a few months later.

The Princess was suspicious of all those shared experiences. She did not want her husband's old cronies around. Perhaps it was time for a new start. Perhaps Diana's resentment of those who had shared the Prince's life before her was understandable.

Even so, it was sad.

# Bobo

It is something of an 'in joke' in Royal circles to remark that the Queen has the commonsense mentality of a Scottish railwayman's daughter. This is not as daft as it sounds. The 'power behind the throne' at Buckingham Palace *is* a commonsense, Scottish railwayman's daughter – Miss Margaret Macdonald, born 1904, and affectionately called Bobo by all the Royal Family. Officially she is the Queen's maid and head dresser. Privately she is much more than that. Bobo is a true loving and loyal friend though, steeped as she is in Royal etiquette, she would never presume to describe herself in such a way.

She has always been exceedingly formal and correct. The Queen and the Royal Family may call her Bobo, but she is Miss Macdonald to everyone else. Palace staff would never dream of calling her Bobo to her face, any more than anyone would call the Queen Lilibet – her pet name.

In the sixty-odd years that she has been at the Queen's side nobody has come within an inch of getting her job or usurping her power. Even at her great age she still guards against anyone getting too near the Queen – whom she considers very much as her property.

She is probably the one person who can and will say anything to the Queen that she thinks she ought to know. It will be Bobo who would mention with great honesty if perhaps the Queen has not put up a perfect appearance on TV or if a dress does not suit her – there are times when she speaks devastatingly frankly.

Bobo has little contact with Prince Philip. Like many of the women family retainers who have devoted their lives to Royalty,

Miss Macdonald has always faintly resented the presence of her mistress's husband. He in turn will try and keep her firmly in her place. He believes her role is to open the curtains in the morning and let the dogs in – tasks she has performed every morning for many, many years since long before Prince Philip of Greece chanced upon the scene.

But then in the Queen's life of duty Bobo has been there for much, much longer than the Duke of Edinburgh. She is still an enormous influence on the Monarch and probably knows her better than anyone else in the world.

When the Queen was born, her first nanny was a Mrs Clara Knight who had also been nanny to the Queen Mother.

The Queen was no more than a few months old when Mrs Knight hired a new teenage nursery maid. She was to assist in the pale blue nursery at their house in Bruton Street, Mayfair, where the infant Princess Elizabeth lived with her parents, the Duke and Duchess of York.

The new recruit to the Royal household was Margaret Macdonald, a small, plain-speaking young woman, born in Scotland just north of Inverness. Her father was a Scottish gardener who later became a railway worker. Margaret was too long a word for the baby Princess Elizabeth to say, and in the Royal tradition of giving affectionate nicknames, Margaret Macdonald became Bobo.

She was an immediate success with the family and when Princess Margaret was born in 1930, Mrs Knight found herself heavily involved with the new infant, so Margaret Macdonald took over the care of the young Elizabeth.

She has been caring for her ever since. And when those close to the Queen remark on matters such as Her Majesty's thrift and her practicality they are noticing good Scottish qualities she learned from Bobo.

The Queen's affection for her is both enormous and understandable. When the Princess was a child, they even shared the same bedroom. During the war, they slept in the same room in the air-raid shelter under Windsor Castle, and until a few years ago when Bobo's frail bones kept breaking, she accompanied the Queen where ever she went.

In the library at Windsor one of the Queen's schoolgirl essays, tied with pink ribbon, has been kept for posterity. It is entitled:

The Coronation, 12 May 1937.
To Mummy and Papa.
In memory of their Coronation.
From Lilibet by herself.

And it is mostly about Bobo. The little Princess wrote: 'I leapt out of bed and so did Bobo. We put on dressing gowns and shoes and Bobo made me put on an eiderdown as it was so cold and we crouched in the window looking on to a cold misty morning . . . Every now and then we were hopping in and out of bed looking at the bands and the soldiers. At six o'clock Bobo got up and instead of getting up at my usual time I jumped out of bed by half past seven. . . .'

All her life, Bobo has been the face the Queen sees first every day. There is a joke that says Bobo is the only person who regularly has the opportunity of saying, 'Arise, your Majesty'. She still wakes her mistress each weekday morning, taking in a cup of tea and a plate of biscuits which have been handed to her by the Queen's footman. No male servants are permitted to enter the Queen's bedroom.

There is an exception to this daily routine. On Bobo's birthday, the Queen will take her maid an early-morning cup of tea.

Margaret Macdonald has been with the Queen at every sad, happy and dramatic moment in her life. She was in charge at Clarence House when Prince Charles was born in November 1948. She was with her mistress at Treetops in Kenya when the Queen's father, King George VI, died in 1952. Bobo and Prince Philip's valet at the time, John Dean, were two of the first to know that the young Princess had become Queen. They were sitting on a doorstep cleaning shoes when the Princess's detective came to convey the calamitous news that was to change all their lives.

Bobo carried on cleaning her mistress's shoes. There wasn't anything else to be done.

Her worst moment came later that morning when the new Queen came out to chat, not yet knowing the dreadful news. She had been fishing, had managed a better catch than Prince Philip and was feeling pleased with herself. Bobo knew it was not her place to tell her of the King's death, though probably no one would have done it better – apart from Philip, who's sad duty it was.

Royalty never travel without mourning clothes. Just in case. It was Bobo who had packed the black coat and hat in which the Queen returned to Britain. And it was Bobo who helped her dress, and who was probably the only person, other than Prince Philip, who witnessed the new Queen's tears.

She, too, was at her mistress's side at the Coronation in Westminster Abbey. At one point in the long ceremony, the young Queen was given time to rest in a retiring room at the Abbey. A small picnic of sandwiches and coffee had been prepared at the Palace and taken to the Abbey. The Queen and the Duke shared this historic meal with Bobo and the Duke's valet who, coincidently was another Macdonald, though not a relative of Bobo.

For many years Bobo has looked like an older version of the Queen. This is not that surprising when you discover that her hair is set by the Queen's hairdresser and her clothes are made by the same dressmakers. When the Royal hairdresser, Charles Martin, has finished attending to the Queen's coiffure at Buckingham Palace, he pops upstairs and attends to Bobo's.

There is much the same arrangement with clothing. Bobo makes all the appointments for the Royal couturiers and has considerable say in choice of style and fabric, and they make her clothes as well. If Bobo is unwell, dressmakers are forced to write to the Queen's Page for an appointment – a successful but slower method which doesn't carry quite the same cachet. Bobo was influential in the choice of the Queen's most recent designer, John Anderson, who used to work at Hartnell. Until his death, Hartnell, was for many years was the Queen's designer and he and Bobo were good friends. Anxious to help any Hartnell protégé, she organised a meeting between Anderson and the Queen, and Anderson made the Queen a striking blue dress for her 1988 visit to Spain.

Bobo takes a genuine interest in fashion and has always been particular about her own appearance. She is now and always has been, a remarkably elegant woman. Bobo may be an old family retainer, but she does not look like one. She owns a very fine fur coat which came from the Queen's furrier. It has her name embroidered on the lining and she is wont to leave it open so that this can be spotted.

Although she has devoted her life to Royalty, Bobo has received much devotion in return from the Queen. It is many a long year since Bobo went anywhere except in one of the chauffeur-driven Royal Fords.

Likewise, although she is a member of Palace staff and not part of the higher-ranking Royal Officials or Household, she has always used the Palace front entrance. She is not obliged like so many Palace servants to make her exits and entrances through the side door. She is untouched by modern security, vehemently refusing to carry one of the new Palace security passes. These are a must for everyone else from the most senior member of the Household to the newest housemaid. Bobo will have nothing to do with them.

The Royals strive to shroud themselves in mystery, and Bobo has successfully created this same mystery for herself – with rather more success. This remarkable woman who knows the Queen so well is largely unknown to the public. To Royal staff she is a living legend and treated warily by her colleagues because of her influence with the Queen. In upstairs-downstairs terms, she gets the same kind of preferential treatment below stairs as her mistress does in the Royal quarters, upstairs.

The Queen's concern for Bobo is touching. There are two footmen whose duties are to look after the Queen, the corgis and assist her Page. They are also there to look after Bobo and make sure she is properly accompanied on all journeys when the Court moves to Windsor, Balmoral and Sandringham. They also see that she never has to carry anything heavy – including the Queen's jewel case – which is officially her responsibility. But she is never parted from a special brown leather dressing case which contains all the Queen's make-up. This is definitely Bobo's responsibility and she will not let anyone else touch it.

She has two assistant dressers to help with her duties, Miss Peggy Hoath, who was once a seamstress with Norman Hartnell the Queen's dressmaker, and Miss May Prentice, a Scotswoman who worked for the late Princess Royal and moved to the Palace after her death. It is assumed that Miss Hoath will take over one day, but for the moment Bobo is still very much in charge, though her great age is beginning to tell. She will still accompany the Queen on the August Western Isles cruise, but once Britannia has arrived at Aberdeen and she has supervised the unpacking, the Queen flies her home to join her sister for her own holiday. These days Bobo prefers Venice to Balmoral.

In the 1970s the Royal Family decided to have a blitz on expenses at Sandringham and also to modernise various aspects. The Comptroller of the Royal Household decreed that in future none of the staff would be served meals in their rooms. Everyone would have to come downstairs to the staff dining-room and serve themselves. And that included Bobo.

She was outraged and promptly acquired a cold. A very bad cold it was, too. One that went on and on. She was much too poorly to visit the dining-room, and her meals had to be delivered to her room by one of her two assistant dressers. Her cold lingered until the Comptroller capitulated, accepting that he was beaten.

Today Bobo is the only one of the staff whose food is served in her own room. And when travelling, she is the first person to be served her food – after the Queen. This is on the Queen's personal instructions.

One thing that did annoy her in her younger days was that meals for the Royal Nanny, Mabel Anderson, were delivered to the nursery and served on Royal nursery silver. Bobo's came from the staff kitchen, and was served on china. There was always a degree of rivalry between the two women, but Miss Anderson left the Palace long ago, and Bobo has reigned supreme ever since. There was also great rivalry between her and Suckling and Field, the women who dressed the Queen Mother for many years. Neither of them were as grand as Miss Macdonald. She is undoubtedly the grandest lady's maid on earth.

Bobo has rarely made a mistake in her long working life though once she misread the jewellery programme list which is furnished by the Lord Chamberlain's office for any special occasion. She missed 'Tiara' and failed to pack even one of the twenty or so that the Queen owns. Deeply embarrassed she had to borrow one from a lady-in-waiting. What made it worse was that the Queen rarely travels without a tiara – just in case.

Another embarrassing moment happened before the Queen ascended the throne and while she was staying at Birkhall in Balmoral for the summer holiday. Prince Philip had invited his private secretary, Michael Parker, and his wife for the weekend. Eileen Parker went to change for dinner and found her evening wear neatly laid out, but no sign of her nightgown. A flustered Bobo had to explain that she had tried to iron it and had made a huge scorchmark right through the middle. Mrs Parker's nightgown was made of nylon. A fabric, no doubt, with which Bobo was none too well acquainted.

She does not work at weekends anymore. When the Queen leaves for Windsor in the Royal Rover after lunch on Friday, Bobo sweeps out of the Palace gates in a Royal Ford, and is driven just a few hundred yards down the Mall to her home, a little grace and favour dwelling in Marlborough House Mews. She shares this with her sister, Ruby, and her brother-in-law, and spends most weekends there, travelling to Windsor only when the Court is there for Ascot Week or the Easter Court. In fact, she goes, 'only when Windsor is properly run' as she puts it. But those who know her believe that she only really considers home to be where the Queen is.

Bobo never married. She was not lacking in opportunities as a young women, and there were men in her life. But had she married, she would have had to leave her mistress and say goodbye to what is a privileged life. Her sister, Ruby, who cared for Princess Margaret for many years, did marry and gave up her job as a Royal dresser. But the dedicated Bobo has always been wedded to her career.

Her unique job has given her a fascinating life. Wherever the

Queen has travelled, Bobo has travelled too. There are few places in the world she has not seen. At Government Houses all over the world whenever Royalty visit, the first question that local staff used to whisper was: 'How is Miss Macdonald?' She is the top backstairs Royal and, as such, a source of fascination to all her colleagues.

For years her age made no difference to her appetite for travel and Royal tours. The first time she was ever left behind was in 1974 when the Queen was visiting Australia. Bobo had fallen and broken a bone. Everyone felt that in the circumstances the trip would be too much for an elderly woman, so it was decided that she should remain in England.

She was apparently most indignant, protesting that she would manage perfectly well; and was furious at being left behind for six weeks with nothing to do and without her mistress. When Prime Minister Edward Heath's political confrontation with the miners brought the Queen home early, Bobo saw it plainly as an Act of God arranged entirely for her benefit.

'There you are,' she said to the Chef, 'the first time the Queen's has ever had to go away without me and now she's back. I knew it would all go wrong if I wasn't there.'

On a later trip when Bobo had damaged her shoulder, the Queen thought it would be good for her to recuperate on the Western Isles cruise. Several sailors carefully carried Bobo aboard the Royal Yacht while all the time she insisted that she was perfectly all right, thank you. She wanted to go ashore on the day-trips, but, much to her chagrin, the Admiral in charge put his foot down, and she was left behind.

Bobo is always given preferential treatment aboard Britannia and is the only staff member whose cabin is completely private. Nobody else is allowed to travel in it. When she is not on board it is locked and not used. It is a particularly attractive cabin – painted white – and with a large window above her bed. Her pretty sitting room is on the next deck, furnished in chintz.

She has her own steward to look after her, and gives pleasant little parties where the steward will serve punch and to which the staff hope to be asked. It is considered a great honour to be invited by Miss Macdonald – who knows, she might put in a good word with the Queen!

She will come down to eat on the yacht and has her own corner table with her own chair. The Queen and the Duke's Pages usually sit with her and anyone who is asked to join them considers the invitation to be an honour.

When the Queen is on holiday at Sandringham, Bobo goes too and it is a treat for the senior staff to be asked for drinks with her. She has a most comfortable little set of rooms, and is the only staff member to have a coal fire.

She inspires awe among the other staff. When she was younger and went to the staff dances at Balmoral, the housemaids and the footmen reacted in the same way as they might for the Queen. Everyone would be whispering, 'Have you heard? Miss Macdonald's coming down.'

On the anniversary of her fifty years of Royal service, the Queen had a special commemorative present made for her by Garrard, the Crown jewellers. Mr Summers, the director of the jewellery firm, was sent for and smuggled in and out of the Palace behind Bobo's back to help the Queen choose from various designs. The final gift was a brooch made in the shape of a flower. It has twenty-five diamonds which represent the crown and twenty-five gold stamens which represent the good that Bobo has brought to the Queen's life.

There is even more telling evidence of the Queen's great regard for her. Bobo was awarded the MVO (Member of the Victorian Order), an honour only given for personal service to the Monarch.

When the Queen announced her intentions her officials pointed out that the MVO was not for ordinary staff, but for members of the Queen's Household or her Officials.

The Queen was solemnly reminded that staff were traditionally given the lesser Royal Victoria Medal. Therefore to give the MVO to Miss Macdonald, dresser and maid, could be setting an embarrassing precedent.

The Queen said it could and would be awarded. And it was. Bobo's luggage reads in bold lettering, Miss Margaret Macdonald, MVO.

She is the only member of the Queen's staff to be so honoured.

# On Stage At The Royal Court

Probably the worst problem about being on stage at the real-life Royal Court is that the role can be so personally restricting and, furthermore, stultifyingly boring.

Princess Margaret, a woman disappointed by life, has been bored with it for years but has learned to use it to her own advantage. Prince Philip has never come to terms with many of the restrictions of being Royal and probably now never will. The Princess Royal, once the most rebellious and rude members of the family has, after many years of sullen behaviour, at last found her niche with a proper job. She works tirelessly for the Save the Children Fund. But nothing will alter her irritation that, as daughter of the Queen, she cannot live an entirely private life.

The Princess of Wales and the Duchess of York, still comparative newcomers to the Royal firm, have been allocated jobs carefully chosen for their glamour or sympathy factors. Diana usually works with children, the sick, or old folk with whom she has an instant rapport. She is also good at (and secretly enjoys) outshining stars on glitzy occasions. Even so, that unmistakable distant look and petulant droop to the mouth that says, 'What the hell am I doing here?' is occasionally inclined to darken Diana's pretty face. The difficulty with coming to Royalty as opposed to being born to it is that the novelty quickly wears off.

These days Diana has almost mastered the royal art of hiding boredom, but not quite. At the Highland Games in September 1988 she made no secret that tossing the caber did not exactly enthrall her. She might have enjoyed it more had Prince William been along, but the Prince of Wales had put his foot down. William was left at home because they couldn't take the risk that he would misbehave. So the Princess, perhaps by way of protest, left a considerable gap between her chair and her husband's – the gap that young William would have filled.

'When the Princess first married she was overawed by her position,' a former member of her Household says. 'So much so she didn't take in all that was going on around her. But now she is more relaxed and wants to know about everything and everybody.'

But there are certain things the Princess finds extremely tedious. Polo holds little interest for Diana. She doesn't mind standing about on a polo field if it can be combined with work, such as helping one of her charities. Unadulterated horse-talk, however, leaves her cold and her eyes glaze over when dinner party conversation revolves around hunting and the day's sport. Family shooting parties at Sandringham used to be quite enjoyable for the Princess but recent photographs of William and Harry out with the guns, and criticism of her allowing them to join in such activities, upset her and she no longer allows the children out when there might be cameras around.

'Diana can be such a bore,' Princess Anne could be heard muttering at a Sandringham shooting party early in 1989. Anne was complaining that a shortage of beaters might spoil the day's shoot, and Diana and the children could have helped. 'If you don't want to come at least let me take the children,' Anne suggested. Diana's reply was – shall we say – pithy?

The Duchess of York, still a comparatively new Royal Family member, appears to be thoroughly enjoying herself most of the time. But even her exuberance was quelled when photographers followed her and her husband on to the ski-slopes during a private weekend. She is learning that there is no such thing as a private life for a member of the Royal Family. Andrew says, 'When you are in a public place, you are fair game, but in a private place it is an intrusion.'

We are fortunate that of the Royal Family, it is the most senior three who accept being Royal for what it is – an important job and one that they do well. In all their public lives neither the Queen nor the Queen Mother has ever put a foot wrong, said the wrong thing, or offended a soul. Both are consummate professionals, magnificent masters of their roles. The Prince of Wales grows daily in stature, an uncertain past is behind him. He has had struggles with self-doubts and introspection, but now he is confident enough to do what the best of Princes should do – speak for the people. Trained for the job by his mother, he is very much a chip off the old block. Even at times of doubt he has always striven to please to the best of his ability. Like the Queen, he steadfastly resolves never to let the boredom show.

The Queen Mother cheerfully admits to never having been bored in her life. This comes because of her enchanting temperament and an insatiable interest in life and everything and everyone around her. She also had the great good fortune to have a truly happy marriage. She and her Bertie courted for two years. There were no doubts in his mind, but the young Lady Elizabeth Bowes-Lyon wanted to be sure that the Royal role and the loss of all personal freedom were pressures that she could bear. In the end, she could not do without her Bertie and happily for us all she accepted the young Duke of York. The Smiling Duchess instantly became one of the best-loved members of the Royal Family.

Today she has been a widow for longer than she was a wife. King George VI was only fifty-six when he died in February, 1952. He adored his wife and mighty though he was, her word was his command.

He used to enjoy lingering over the port while the ladies retired to the drawing-room. He and his Queen did not take coffee after their meals. They preferred tea. When his wife felt that he had been away for long enough and she was ready for her cuppa, she would draw a teapot on a piece of paper and ask her Page to take it to the King in the dining-room. His Majesty would come through immediately when the command came.

The Queen Mother never had to suffer the same constrictions that are placed on the Queen today. Because she is not and never was the Monarch she has more opportunity to reveal her charming, natural self.

A Palace footman tells the small but telling story of riding on the back of the Queen Mother's coach at the opening of one Royal Show. The Queen Mother, guest of honour at this big yearly agricultural event, shared her open carriage with Sir Dudley Forwood, the Honorary Director.

It was a blustery day but that did not stop the Royal guest wearing one of her spectacular hats and Sir Dudley was convinced that it was going to blow away. His hand kept creeping tentatively towards the brim, and finally after one particularly violent gust of wind he could stand the suspense no longer. He anchored his hand on the top of the feathered creation and held it very firmly in place.

The Queen Mother turned her ravishing smile on him. 'Oh, Sir

Dudley!' she sighed. 'In a more gracious age I would have made you my comptroller of hats.'

The Queen is not permitted even such innocent remarks and she is certainly not allowed public opinions on matters more serious. Even at her own private dinner parties with friends if the conversation turns to religion or politics or anything controversial, she begins to fuss with the corgis who are always at her feet under the table. Prince Philip calls this, Lilibet's dog defence.

It is the Queen who gets the worst of the yawning chasms of boredom that Royal routine can bring. It is she who must every year attend an average of sixty State lunches and dinners as well as three banquets. She doesn't have to shake hands with everyone but she has to entertain a total of around 30,000 people each year at three separate Buckingham Palace garden parties and another 4000 in the Palace of Holyroodhouse in Edinburgh. She also presents 2000 honours to complete strangers in the course of the year and holds dozens of audiences for politicians and foreign dignitaries.

The silver lining in this particular cloud is that most of them have to walk backwards out of the room so as not to turn their back on her presence. At State dinners as she makes her way in procession to the State dining-room, the Lord High Steward and the Lord Chamberlain have to lead her in, walking backwards. Not unnaturally this is a manoeuvre that those unfortunate enough to find themselves stuck with, make with extreme caution, praying that they will not fall over backwards and make fools of themselves.

And sometimes it is equally hard for the Queen, who has a highly developed sense of humour, not to smile. Familiarity hasn't divested the scene of its comic potential. No man is at his dignified best walking backwards. For such delicate moments, the Queen has adopted a stern, unsmiling look which is really no more than a desperate attempt to keep a straight face.

She herself tells a story about her great-great-grandmother, Queen Victoria, who was reputed never to be amused. The Queen says that history has got it wrong and that in fact she frequently was. When something ridiculous happened to lighten life, Victoria would sit there stony-faced and stern. Inside, she was hysterical with mirth which was obvious to those who knew her because small, slow tears would be trickling down her face.

Our Queen manages to achieve the same effect without the tears. But once in private, she and her immediate family will all be in hysterics as she brilliantly mimics the posturing and pomposity of those she has to deal with. But never does she show this side of her character in public. One can can hardly blame her. Most of the

Queen's job is so mind-bogglingly dull that if she didn't manage to get a bit of amusement from it, she'd end up waiting for the men in white coats.

For truly stultifying boredom, take investitures. When Her Majesty presents awards the ritual never varies. In one day about 150 loyal subjects arrive at the Palace, both proud and nervous, to be honoured in some way. Perhaps even knighted. Year in, year out nothing changes. While the Queen is busy knighting someone or other, one Page of the Back Stairs stands by holding her handbag (which has nothing much in it), while another holds the ceremonial sword which he carefully and solemnly hands to her Equerry. The Equerry then passes it to the Queen who gently taps the shoulders of the person being knighted with the sword. What she does not do, contrary to popular belief, is intone, 'Arise, Sir . . .'. She merely says a few gracious words of congratulation having already been well briefed by her officials on the background and achievements of the new knight.

On the not-so-rare occasions when someone handicapped receives an honour, Queen Mary's old wheelchair is taken out of store and used for transportation to where the Queen waits.

All the arrangements for these honours ceremonies are made by the Lord Chancellor's office. Each recipient has to be personally presented with his or her award and the presenter is almost always the Queen herself. People expect her to hand them their honour and are usually keenly disappointed if she is not there. Therefore, if the Queen is in Britain, that's who they get. If by chance she is away on a State visit or otherwise out of London, then one of her Counsellors of State takes over. Two Counsellors are always appointed when the Queen goes abroad and they are almost always close members of the family. The Queen Mother was most likely to stand in for her daughter and hand out the honours. Her personal popularity is so great that people were not disappointed she took longer to get through the ceremony. The Queen has an investiture down to a fine art and can hand over 140 medals, insignia, titles, etc. in an hour and ten minutes. The Queen Mother, who does enjoy a little chat, took an hour and a half to perform the same job. Prince Charles is more likely to take over now if his mother is away.

Investitures are, of course, a lot more fun for the Royal Family if the famous are queueing up for their award. The Queen has been overheard to whisper in public places, and particularly at film premieres, 'Look, there is so-and-so'. She enjoys spotting the famous just as much as we enjoy spotting her or her family.

A dreary investiture is one where only doctors, teachers, professors and the like are being honoured – no well-known faces. On one particular day when there were no show business or sporting recipients the Queen, her job done, and her handbag retrieved and back over her arm, came through into the East Gallery and into the State dining-room where footmen closed the doors behind her. As the corgis scampered to greet her and she visibly relaxed she said to the Comptroller: 'Whew! Had I tripped and fallen in there and the Lord Chamberlain had asked if there were a doctor in the house, I'd have been crushed in the stampede!'

A popular name to be honoured was Dick Francis, the author and ex-jockey who received the OBE. The Queen had bumped into him at a literary party and like the true racing addict that she is, said, 'Ah, yes, you used to be my mother's jockey.'

Not a word about his books! But it was not long before he was in the Honours' List.

Privately the Queen states her opinion of some of her subjects quite forcably. She is a pretty good judge of character, and not a few politicians and captains of industry would be dismayed to hear themselves referred to as bonkers or even fools. Fool, though, is about the unkindest thing that she ever says about anyone, and this is tempered to lovable fool if she's referring to someone who is normally in her good books. When she and Princess Margaret were teenagers and the Princess Margaret behaved badly, the Queen's only comment would be to called her sister a ridiculous child. But it was always said fondly.

The Royal Family must be above politics publicly, though not unnaturally they do have their favourite politicians whom they like regardless of their party. Prince Charles, for example, very much liked the distinguished Labour politician James Callaghan.

The Queen had a soft spot for Harold Wilson – not surprisingly since he did steer her through ten years of his premiership. He spent longer at the Tuesday meetings with her than other prime minister and kept her fully informed about what was going on. He also liked the theatre which endeared him to the Queen. He would make pronouncements and do things at odd hours. He picked late Friday night to devalue the pound, but it is on Fridays that come hell or high water the Queen goes to Windsor after lunch between 2.30 and 3.00. The Palace staff couldn't think what was happening. Here it was well after three on a Friday and the Queen was still in her rooms with the Palace lit up like a Christmas tree. Then in swept the Prime Minister to tell the Queen in advance about the dramatic devaluation. Wilson knew how to break the monotony, and the Queen appreciated it.

Willie Hamilton, the tiresome MP who was always rabbiting on about abolishing the Monarchy, will be most disappointed to know that the Royals never even mentioned him.

A Royal duty that actually relieved the boredom was the giving away of the British Empire. When these red dots on the map remain British, they have to be visited periodically by someone from the Royal Family to make it clear that we haven't forgotten all about them, but today there is not much left of the Empire to dispose of.

For a time in the 1960s and 70s, island after far-flung island was being given its independence. Each time a member of the Royal Family flew in to perform the ceremony which usually took place at midnight, symbolic of the dawning of a new day. The officiating Royal, dressed up to the nines, had to stand on a ricketty platform and make a speech on behalf of the Queen. Down came the Union Jack and up went the flag of the new country. And a band played.

Many of the ceremonies were unrelenting comic opera. Prince Charles, who was forever declaring independence somewhere or other, had once to purloin the island's only car – a vintage Morris Minor – while the accompanying procession pedalled along behind like mad on bicycles.

The Gold Coast also provided a bit of light, if embarrassing, comic relief. Prince Charles arrived there to find every woman in the crowds lining the route from the airport was dressed from head to foot in fabric printed all over with pictures of his face. He found it most disconcerting to be greeted with so many replicas of himself.

But he cherished the sight of the big Barbadian lady who was so overcome at seeing him that she was jumping up and down crying: 'Hallelujah! Now I've seen my earthly Prince I'm ready for my heavenly one!'

And in Papua New Guinea, the Prince found that as well as handing over independence he was required to present medals to an array of almost topless ladies.

'Where the hell am I going to put them?' he said appalled at the thought of pinning medals on the narrow covering over the ladies' bosoms. His resourceful valet, who never travelled without a couple of big boxes of safety pins, came up with the answer. He made strings of safety pins and hung the medals in the middle. All the Prince had to do was drop the necklaces neatly over the lady's heads – all embarrassment averted.

There was also an occasional brush with danger. Prince Charles once arrived for a visit to Ghana when, as his Andover of the Queen's Flight was about the land, the entire guard of honour below suddenly took off and sped across the runway. Apparently they had realised at the last minute that they were in the wrong place. Rather than mow them down, the pilot took to the skies again with a roar of engines and at a dizzying angle. It was, said Prince Charles afterwards, quite a hairy moment. On this occasion, the Prince, a skilful pilot who likes to land a plane himself, was not at the controls. He was at the back of the aircraft putting medals on his naval uniform ready to inspect the suicidal guard of honour.

Much nearer home, he along with his two policeman at the time, Paul Officer and John McClean, and his valet, found themselves being driven by a chauffeur from the Royal Mews, who was in something of a hurry. They were making the cross-country run from Eastbourne to Windsor, and the driver, who had perhaps had a few drinks while he was waiting, drove like a lunatic. The two policemen ordered him to slow down, but he raced on, throwing his passengers around in their seats and frightening the life out of all four of them.

Prince Charles was furious and, unusually for him, rang Sir John Miller in the Royal Mews afterwards and complained. The Palace rarely fire anyone. They just rearrange things. The man was merely demoted, but he never drove the Prince again. The valet recalled: 'It gave us all something to talk about for a day or two.'

Another incident that gave them something to talk about took place at Buckingham Palace. An African President arrived in Britain on a State visit with an enormous retinue. This is not unusual with Third World countries. The Royal Family are aware that by way of insurance foreign Presidents sometimes bring with them just about everyone of the slightest importance to prevent a coup d'état in their absence. Prince Charles had been for his morning swim in the Palace pool and was running back to his own rooms. Suddenly out of a door popped a black gentleman holding a bundle of clothing.

'You press,' he demanded, pushing the clothes into the Prince's hands. 'Certainly, Sir,' said the Prince, and continued to run down the corridor until he found a footman to pass them on to. 'Guess what happened,' he said to his valet when he got back upstairs. 'I nearly got your job.'

He caused a bit of a stir when he was in the Navy by growing a beard – what the Navy call a full set. The Queen loved it. She said that it made him look the spitting image of his great-grandfather, George V. Princess Margaret couldn't bear it. The beard had to go when he was installed in the Order of the Bath. He wore the uniform of a

Welsh Guards' Colonel and the Guards are not permitted beards. He compromised with a moustache which made him look a touch caddish, but eventually that went, too.

Prince Charles can always take a joke against himself. He is not remotely pompous as proved in his fortieth birthday speech when with great good humour he talked about chatting to the flower-beds, cleverly mocking those in the press who had been calling him barmy. He was in a Birmingham tram shed at the time.

'Only the other day,' the Prince said, 'I was enquiring of a bed of old-fashioned roses, who were forced to listen to my demented ramblings on the meaning of the universe as I sat cross-legged in the lotus position in front of them. I was enquiring what would happen on my birthday in a Birmingham tram shed.

'"A tram shed?" they all replied, totally aghast.

'"Yes," I said. "A tram shed."

'"But can't they find anything more salubrious in Birmingham?" asked one, who had by now lost her petals and was looking decidedly the worse for wear.

'"Apparently not. They seem to have knocked most of it down. They can't find anything else."

'At this point a row of prize Welsh leeks, cocky little things, who were lurking nearby in a vegetable patch, chipped in to say the shed would be filled with semi-naked Kalahari bushmen doing a fertility dance and a troupe or two of Tibetan monks who had proceeded from Saffron Walden by levitation, with advance copies of the tabloid newspapers which would be strewn in my path.'

Speaking to the Company of Master Mariners in London early in 1989 he again took the micky out of himself explaining how he had once succeeded in anchoring on an underwater telephone cable between Holyhead and Ireland.

'The problem was getting off it again, because I had terrible visions as we tried to pull it up and down that all the telegraph poles in County Donegal were all going. . . .' He used his fingers to illustrate the poles slowly tumbling to the ground.

Charles also told of the time he caused outrage among the admirals after he was 'wheeled' off minehunter Bronington 'with a lavatory seat around my neck'.

He was asked how it was possible to be promoted to Captain with such a record. He replied: 'The answer is that it pays to know the right people, i.e. the Lord High Admiral.'

The Lord High Admiral is the Queen.

But sometimes he has a curious innocence about modern life which his wife does not share. A few years ago he and Diana went to

76

dinner with friends in London and after the meal they played Trivial Pursuit. The game was new to the Prince, and one of his questions was, 'What does Private Eye call the Queen?' The Prince hadn't a clue, which his knowledgeable wife thought hilarious. 'Don't be silly, Charles,' she said. 'They call her Brenda.'

There was a time when he was into practical joking. When he was with the RAF at Cranwell in the 1970s he issued a directive that all airmen must leave their boots at the porter's lodge because the boot issue was wrong. A puzzled porter arrived to find he couldn't get into his lodge for boots. Later the Prince owned up.

He also finds impersonations of himself a hoot. Prince Edward is known to perform a brilliant one.

'Being the Prince of Wales does have its funny moments,' Charles once said. 'Only the other day I was chatting with a fellow who suddenly stared at me intently and said, "Do you know, meeting you is just like meeting Mike Yarwood".'

Prince Charles has long realised that to make fun of one's self occasionally is a safe and sure way to the nation's heart. He recalls a day when he was riding in Great Windsor Park. He had stopped to admire the view when a small boy appeared and stood staring intently at him, head cocked to one side. 'Ere,' he said, 'are you Mark Phillips?'

'No,' said the Prince. 'So sorry.'

'Oh, all right then,' said the lad with a disappointed shrug, and wandered off.

It was an anecdote that would have delighted the Queen. She adores jokes and also likes hearing a bit of gossip. She likes to know what is going on in every corner of her various homes. And her immediate servants save up all the latest chit-chat for her. But what her staff pass on in the privacy of her own sitting-room goes no further and there is certainly no feed-back to any of her informants about what her own family are doing.

The Queen Mother, though loving a chat, cannot abide gossip and refuses to listen to it; but Prince Philip, like his wife, is not averse to knowing what is going on in the Palace corridors.

One morning he remarked to his valet that he had not seen one of the footmen for a while.

'I'm afraid, Sir, he was fired,' his valet reported.

'For what?' the frowning Duke demanded to know.

The valet lowered his voice.

'I'm afraid, Sir, they found him in bed with one of the house-maids.'

'And they fired him for that?' exploded the Duke, who has been known to grumble about the number of gags around the Palace. 'The man should have been given a medal.'

There was a time when the Queen employed a somewhat eccentric cook-housekeeper at one of her smaller Scottish houses. The elderly Scotswoman was not an ideal choice, but the house is remote, freezing in winter, and anyone willing to staff it is hard to find. The woman survived in the job because in spite of a weakness for the bottle, when on form, and sober, she was an extremely good cook.

One year Prince Philip took a shooting party to the house just before Christmas. The cook-housekeeper was given the menu for the weekend, and told to make a chocolate mousse laced with Glenfiddich malt whisky for a pudding the following day.

When the Royal party came down for breakfast they found the mousse made, as ordered, and the housekeeper on her knees on the kitchen floor, rolling out the pastry for a luncheon pie. An empty Glenfiddich bottle lay beside her.

At the time the Royal party considered it hilarious. The incident gave the Duke and his guests something different to talk about. But once Christmas was over, stern commonsense prevailed and the Master of the Household sent her on her way.

Many years ago, the Queen Mother also had a footman who enjoyed a drink. He caused a rumpus when Princess Margaret, her two children and their Nanny were staying with the Queen Mother at Hillingdon House near Sandringham. Trouble began when the Princess and her mother came home from the afternoon shoot to the sounds of loud banging from upstairs in the direction of the nursery.

'Is everything all right, Nanny?' Princess Margaret called. It was not. Nanny had barricaded herself into the nursery along with her small charges Lord Linley and Sarah Armstrong-Jones. The banging was a very drunken footman trying to get in to give her a drink she didn't want. Hearing the Princess's voice he fled with some speed.

Realising the coast was clear, Nanny opened the door and red with rage, heatedly aired her grievances about the footman's behaviour.

Princess Margaret listened with great sympathy, and shaking her head went to get a drink herself. As her mother's Page was pouring her a whisky and water she told him what had happened.

'I wouldn't mind,' she concluded, 'but he knows that Nanny only likes sherry. Can you believe, he was trying to force a whisky on her!'

This same footman was once discovered, by the Queen Mother,

passed out in the hall but there was great tolerance of human frailty and he kept his job.

Another of the Queen Mother's staff, one of her dressers who enjoyed her food and drink, was once following her mistress off an aircraft, carrying the Royal hat-box. The clasp came undone, but instead of one of the Queen Mother's splendidly befeathered hats, a bottle of gin came tumbling out, breaking as it hit the tarmac. The dresser was most upset, not so much because the Queen Mother had seen the secret contents of her hat-box but at the dreadful waste of a full bottle of gin.

When the Royal Family visit friends, their ever-present detectives are usually left in the kitchen with nothing to do until it is time to see their charges home. The detectives get fed, they get given cups of tea and sometimes they get a drink or two.

It was the drink or two that once caused a problem for one of the Queen Mother's detectives. On the way back to Royal Lodge from London he was sitting in the front with the chauffeur while the Queen Mother made herself comfortable in the back. As the car nosed its way through the rush-hour traffic, he gently nodded off. Suddenly the driver stopped the car with a jerk at a red light. Startled, the detective woke and automatically leapt to get himself out on to the pavement. Then, in a moment of pure farce, he opened the rear door with a flourish and stood to attention waiting to help the Queen Mother out.

Her Majesty smiled gently at him from the back seat. 'Shouldn't we perhaps go on a little further?' she suggested. 'To Royal Lodge, maybe?'

The detective took a look around him and realised he was standing in the middle of Hammersmith Broadway. Covered in confusion, he leapt back into the front seat. When telling the story himself later, he said with relief and gratitude, 'She never mentioned another word about it.'

Neither the Queen nor her mother goes on about things. When new staff come to the Palace it is necessary to break them in gently to the sight of Royalty. Otherwise they stare. And they are not allowed to do too much until they are used to seeing the Queen face to face. A brand new, very young footman confronted by the Queen for the first time turned brilliant scarlet and dropped the superb china plates he was holding. Every one of them smashed, and he had been breaking the rules. No footman is supposed to carry more than four priceless plates at once or six in an emergency. He was holding eight. As he stood, drooping with dismay, the Queen smiled at him and said gently, 'Don't worry. Just carry on.' She sees all but she turns a blind eye to small misdemeanours or disasters.

One of the more amusing disasters occurred in the middle of a magnificent State banquet, although it has to be said that it is probably the only time anything has ever gone wrong on such an occasion.

A State banquet, which takes place in the Ballroom of Buckingham Palace, is a theatrical production. The table is laid by the Palace under-butlers and the distance between the solid gold knives and forks is actually measured with a ruler. The room is lit only by candles. Soft music comes from the string section of one of the military bands in a balcony above.

It was in this beautiful setting that disaster struck one unfortunate guest. The Queen, as always, was at the head of the table, with her guest, the President of Austria. The Archbishop of Canterbury, was seated nearby. Opposite him sat a Dame Commander of the Order of the British Empire who was also a full brigadier in the Army.

The Brigadier, a well-proportioned lady, was wearing an elegant black evening dress, held in place by two thin shoulder straps. On the left side of her dress, she wore the ribbons of her medals. It was these that were to cause her considerable embarrassment.

The serving footman wore full livery, and on the sleeves of his velvet and gilt jacket were five large gold buttons, stamped with the Queen's coat of arms.

As he bent over to serve the Brigadier her vegetables, one of these buttons become entangled with the row of ribbons above her ample bosom. He tried first to extricate himself while holding the silver tray of vegetables in his hand. This proved impossible. With difficulty he found a spot on the crowded table to divest himself of the dish. The lady brigadier kept her cool and did her best to help him and between them they finally untangled button and strap.

Relieved, but red face and flustered, the footman bent to retrieve his vegetable dish. Fate was not on his side. Or indeed the Brigadier's. Another button caught in her other shoulder strap.

This time the lady lost her cool. Dismayed (as well she might be), she pulled away from the footman just as he pulled away from her. The strap snapped, closely followed by its fellow. Now in a panic, she pushed herself back from the table and with the same movement, pushed herself out of her dress. There was a terrible hush in the immediate vicinity. The Archbishop stared at his plate as if the secret of the universe were written there. The Queen determinedly continued her conversation with the President of Austria. The President of Austria seemed somewhat distracted.

For once the Royal rule that no one leaves the table before the Queen was broken and the lady hurriedly left in search of a couple of safety-pins.

She still tells the tale – as do the Royal Family.

It is not just the Queen who is brilliant at controlling her laughter, so are the rest of the family with the possible exception of Princess Diana who is occasionally afflicted with terrible giggles. On one famous occasion she was standing in for the Queen, taking a salute at the Sovereign's Parade at the Military Academy, Sandhurst. Nerves got the better of her and she couldn't stop laughing. To make matters worse, at the end of the ceremony there is a moment when the Adjutant of the College traditionally rides his horse up the steps of the Grand Entrance and right into the building. It was all too much for Diana who simply could not control her hysterical laughter.

Fergie's humour also has a devastating effect on the Princess of Wales and when she first appeared on the scene they spent many a day together dissolved in giggles. In 1986 they made their infamous foray into a top London nightclub, Annabel's, disguised as police-women, mistakenly thinking that Prince Andrew was having his stag night party there. Diana and Fergie, with comedienne Pamela Stephenson and Elton John's ex-wife, Renate, had been dining with the Duchess of Roxburghe at her home. Pamela Stephenson, would you believe, just happened to have several policewoman's outfits in her car, and suggested that they all dress up. Diana had been complaining that she was tired and would go home, but she perked up at the suggestion and Fergie leapt at the idea. It was naughty, exciting and potentially so over-the-top for a Princess and a Duchess-to-be that it caught their imaginations.

From the moment they struggled into the clothes, hats and wigs, Diana was shaking with laughter. She donned a pair of glasses to complete the disguise and together with Fergie and their show business friends – plus, of course, a rather nervous detective – drove to the nightclub in Mayfair.

Fergie, more used to this kind of jolly jape, was able to keep a straight face. For Diana it was impossible. Eventually, of course, their unsubtle disguise caused so much attention that they were recognised. Convulsed with laughter they left the club, Diana doing a passable imitation of a Charlie Chaplin walk across Berkeley Square as they made their way back to the waiting car.

In the normal way, royalty do not laugh out loud in public. Nor do they let it be known that they might have spotted anything untoward. Every Boxing Day it is a Royal tradition that the men go shooting in the morning, and the ladies join them for lunch – usually in a village hall on the Royal estates. One year they picked upon a hall in the middle of the Home Park at Windsor for the lunchtime meeting. The food as usual was transported from the Castle in the special food boxes that Prince Philip designed to keep hot food hot and cold food cold, and the footmen were busy setting up the tables. One of them went to take a look at the lavatories to make sure they were suitably clean for the Royal needs.

They were not. He was horrified to find that the walls were covered with some particularly crude graffiti. Another footman made a desperate dashed back to the Castle for scrubbing brushes, bleach and cleaning materials and they all set to work in the time that remained before the Royal party arrived. But unfortunately the graffiti was stubborn. Nothing would shift it. The offending words and drawings remained.

When the Royal party arrived, the Queen Mother went into the ladies' room first. The footmen couldn't help noticing that she remained there for rather a long time but she came out absolutely expressionless. One by one the other Royal ladies paid their visits followed by their lady guests. The footmen waited for some reaction, anything from shock-horror to amusement, but all the ladies were resolutely poker-faced. There was much speculation as to whether they might have compared notes later.

Because Royal lives are so rigidly ordered, set in a routine that barely changes from year to year, any diversion however trivial is considered enormous and jolly fun. The Royal Family loves anything that breaks the monotony.

On one occasion, in the middle of a film show on the Royal Yacht, the Queen and her family were sitting, as always, in the front row in Britannia's private cinema. The yacht, top-heavy from all the extra superstructure she carries, was rocking and rolling, battling through heavy seas on her way to Scandinavia where the Royal Family were to visit Lord Mountbatten's sister, the Queen of Sweden.

Suddenly the entire front row of seats collapsed. The family were tumbled to the carpet. If necessary, they can create merry hell when things don't go their way, but on this occasion they roared laughter, picked themselves up and dusted themselves down.

They had enjoyed the diversion.

Another diversion which broke with routine was when Sandringham House had to be renovated. There was a time when Sandringham – which Edward VII called 'that voracious white elephant' – desperately needed refurbishing.

Bowing to the inevitable, the work was put in progress and

eventually some £400,000 of the Queen's own Privy Purse was spent on the house. The work, including demolishing ninety-one of the 270 rooms, rendered the house uninhabitable. But this did not mean that the Royal Family, who always spend New Year's Eve and most of January in Norfolk, were about to change their routine. They crammed themselves into Wood Farm, a much smaller house on the Sandringham Estate.

There simply wasn't room for everyone, so Princess Anne and her husband Mark Phillips arrived with a caravan. They parked this outside the back door and wired it up to the kitchen for electricity. They had their meals inside the house and at night, retired through the kitchen to the caravan to sleep and, it seemed, thoroughly enjoyed themselves.

New Year's Eve at Sandringham House is always a high spot during the Royal year. The Queen is on holiday, in her own home and with all her immediate family around her. The festival is special to her. There is always a punch brewed by one of the Pages who has a knack for it. This is served at midnight, *Auld Lang Syne* is played on the record player and sung by all, just like any other family in the land. The youngest, dark-haired footman comes through the front door and hands pieces of coal for good luck to the Royal ladies in the Scottish, first-footing tradition.

The Royal Family used to play parlour games on these occasions, and one New Year's Eve they were playing Blind Man's Buff. The Queen Mother was blindfolded and searching for quarry to kiss. She heard a sound behind her, and turned around to catch a figure in her arms. She felt for the face and soundly kissed it.

A gale of laughter followed. She took off the blindfold to discover that she had warmly kissed the blushing tall, dark footman who had come in through the French windows as their 'first footer'.

One year while Sandringham was uninhabitable and Wood House was packed to bursting, the Queen Mother stayed at Hillingdon House, three miles away. At that time it was the home of her closest friend and Princess Diana's grandmother, Lady Fermoy. For some reason, the Queen Mother decided she wanted to return to Hillingdon early and go to bed. But it wasn't yet even ten o'clock and as a good Scot, she did not want to ignore New Year, nor miss the traditional first footing.

The problem was solved by one of the Pages putting the chiming clocks in the sitting room and every other clock in the house forward two hours. As twelve o'clock chimed the Royal Family wished each other a Happy New Year, the record player was turned on, the footman appeared with the coal and then the Queen Mother went off to Hillingdon House and her bed, leaving the Pages to put the clocks right again and the staff to enjoy New Year at the normal time. From their point of view it was a popular move. They got to drink the punch. It hadn't been ready earlier.

All that unaccustomed discomfort was considered great fun. The Queen even managed to receive the then Governor General of Australia, Sir John Kerr, at Wood Farm. It was perhaps not quite what he might have expected since the entrance to the house is through the kitchen. He waited, somewhat bewildered, while the chef cooked the lunch until the Queen's Page led him out into the hall where Her Majesty was waiting to greet him. Everyone agreed it went off rather well. The Queen can add dignity to any occasion.

Sandringham holds another diversion that is highly popular in Royal circles. To be on the safe side, every January when the Royal Family are in residence, fire practices are held. These are one of the high spots in the six-week winter holiday since they can cause chaos for a couple of days afterwards and even make dinner late – something unheard of in Royal life.

The fire alarm bell usually goes off between 4.30 and 5.30 in the afternoon. This allows time for those who have been out shooting grouse all day to get back into the house.

When the bell clangs, everyone – staff and Royalty alike – must run for safety. Senior staff 'rescue' blankets, meant to represent valuable paintings, jewellery, tapestries or the fur coats that the women aren't already wearing in the freezing Norfolk January weather. The Royal Family's only duty is to rescue themselves. The staff have to congregate on one side of the lawn – the Royal Family and their guests on the other. An Equerry waits to count them and make sure all are present and correct. The Sergeant Footman counts the staff. Apartheid appears to rules even if the house is burning down!

In a little while a fire engine comes clattering in from King's Lynn, well over-staffed by firemen all anxious to get in on the act. They arrange their hoses around the house to prove that they could cope if this were the real thing. That done, everyone can go back into the warmth again.

The firemen get a beer or two before they leave, served to them by the Yeoman of the Cellar. On occasions when the exercise has raised an unusual thirst, the Queen has been known to mutter, 'I dread to think what they would have drunk if the fire had been a real one.'

Lord Mountbatten's home, Broadlands, had, and presumably still has, a very complicated fire alarm system for insurance reasons

which was always being triggered off accidentally. One night Prince
Charles and his Great Uncle were at dinner when the alarm went off.
Bells rang, lights flashed and dutifully everyone went to the front
hall to get out. One of the staff rushed from the kitchens and said:
'Sorry, sir, it's a false alarm, but the firemen are here.'

'We had better tell them it's all right,' Prince Charles said, heading
for the front door.

His Uncle stopped him with an imperious, upraised hand. 'Don't
be silly, Charles,' he said. 'The firemen always go to the tradesmen's
entrance.'

And sure enough, there they were.

# Money Matters

Considering that it is hardly a problem for most of them, the Royal Family have a highly developed sense of the value of money.

The Queen is probably the richest woman in the world and custodian of a Royal ransom of the nation's treasures. Yet she is careful with cash, almost to the point of frugality. She herself goes around switching off unnecessary lights in her own homes like Balmoral and Sandringham where paying the electricity bill is down to her. She also insists that food is not wasted; she keeps her cars until they are a great age and has the bedlinen turned top to tail daily for family, and weekly for staff, to cut down on laundry bills. If anyone is chilly, rather than turn up the central heating, she briskly suggests that they 'put on another sweater'.

When they leave Balmoral after their summer holidays every drop of alcohol left in the cellars comes back with them even if it is only a half bottle. And that half bottle will be carefully recorded in the Drinks Book, kept by the Yeoman of the Cellar. Eventually the Deputy Master of the Household will check on this to make sure that the half-bottles duly arrive safely back at the Palace.

Prince Philip is forever seeking ways to cut down on expenditure, and it is he who has quietly and wisely made Royal Estates pay their own way. Sandringham farms turkeys and ducks and grows apples, blackcurrants and mushrooms. Some of these are produced on the few hundred acres of land the Duke reclaimed from the sea to enlarge the estate. It is interesting to remember that the Duke of Windsor complained bitterly of the Sandringham apples saying:

'I reckon that every apple grown on those trees cost me a shilling each, after I had paid for the cultivation and the staff there.' Prince Philip has changed all that. Even the Royal hobbies of shooting and fishing yield income from the sale of game and salmon, nor is the Queen averse to making money from breeding at the Royal kennels at Sandringham and the Royal stud.

Her horse racing and breeding interests are managed by Lord Caernarvon from the Highclere Stud in Wiltshire. He is responsible for buying, selling and breeding. Up until recently Major Dick Herne was in charge of the training and racing at the West Isley Stables. A man of sixty-eight, he was crippled five years ago in a hunting accident and is now confined to a wheelchair. In the Spring of 1989, Lord Caernarvon's godson, trainer Willie Hastings-Bass, took over from the Major causing some outrage in the racing circles. In the end, the Palace relented. Now the Major and Hastings-Bass share the Crown lease of the stables. The Queen herself is considered one of the world's foremost authorities on horse-flesh. The whole of her racing activities are privately financed – by the sale of brood mares, the sale of horses in training, or by the sale of nominations to one of her stallions. The stables are run on commercial terms and the Queen is one of the most successful owners and breeders of racehorses in the world. She leaves the Queen Mother to concentrate on National Hunt racing. The Queen Mother hates selling her horses, and is not very commercially minded, but the last two years have been very successful and she has had many winners with her horses trained by Fulke Walwyn.

Prince Charles stables his polo ponies at the Royal Mews at Windsor and each pony costs about £3000 a year to keep.

It is perhaps understandable, indeed, commendable, that those born richly Royal have deep respect for money. It is those not born Royal – the outsiders who marry into the family who tend not to have the same regard for cash. While quietly giving away thousands and thousands of pounds to charity, Prince Charles watches the pennies, and grumbles about the price of everything from a bale of hay for his polo ponies down to the appalling expense of Christmas presents. He calls this 'his Scottish meanness'. Princess Diana however is a happy spender. Given the opportunity she will spend money like a drunken sailor – but not necessarily on herself. She is always buying her friends and staff little presents.

This was something of a problem at the start of the marriage when this twenty-year-old girl suddenly found herself able to walk into Harrods without a penny or a credit card in her pocket, buy what she wanted, and tell them to send the bill to the Palace where it would be paid by the Prince's office. But her spendthrift sins came home to haunt her. Though Prince Charles has never written a cheque in his life, he likes to know what is happening to his money and there were recriminations when one of his close officials gave the game away. They no longer row about money, but he does check her bills.

When Sarah Ferguson first met Prince Andrew she didn't even own her own flat. She shared one south of the river in Battersea with a friend. Her family are comfortably off, but not rich. Sarah has a small income from a trust set up by her grandfather but it is her stepmother Susan who has most of the family money, inherited from her landowning father.

Susan and Ronald Ferguson live in a beautiful Georgian farmhouse on an 800-acre estate in Hampshire. This was left to Ronald Ferguson in 1966 by his father. The Major, who spent twenty years in the Household Cavalry on Army pay, denies having much spare cash.

'I gave Sarah a small allowance, that's all,' he insists, 'but she had to work to earn a living. When you're royal, people automatically assume you are rich which certainly isn't true at all.'

When Sarah became royal by marrying Prince Andrew she certainly didn't become rich. Her blue BMW was replaced by a sporty Jaguar XJS but it was leased. Her rented apartment was replaced by a suite in Buckingham Palace which had once been Prince Charles' bachelor quarters. She still had nothing to call truly her own, and she and her husband found their expenses were mounting at a terrifying rate. Their Civil List allowance was increased from £86,500 to £155,400 per annum in 1989 but this had to cover the cost of running their office and paying for staff. A lot of staff – an Equerry, a dresser, a valet, a private secretary, general secretary, and the expenses of two ladies-in-waiting.

General staff at the Palace are paid by the Queen, but at Castlewood House, their temporary country home, cooks and domestics are paid by Andrew and Sarah, who also employ a full-time nanny, Alison Wardley. All of this leaves little for extras. Since the birth of Princess Beatrice, Sarah has had to give up the £25,000 she was earning from her job as a commissioning editor. Andrew earns roughly £20,000 from the navy.

Not surprisingly Fergie began to run up an overdraft. The kind of clothes she now needs are not cheap and she needs a lot of them. Anxious to help, her friends have introduced the Duchess to shops who will lend her clothes and jewellery. The French couture house, Yves St Laurent, came up trumps and immediately 'lent' her some wildly expensive dresses and suits – all provided on a 'temporary' (but usually non-returnable) basis. St Laurent recognised the immense publicity value of the Duchess being seen in his creations and Fergie was delighted with the opportunity to wear them.

'We are only number two and we don't have much money', was one of her constant comments. But Fergie has been brought up in a traditionally English manner where to spend thousands of pounds on frocks – however much money you have – is considered rather bad form. Therefore it seemed a suitable arrangement to borrow rather than to buy them. It also seemed very sensible to take advantage of some of the free holidays offered her and it didn't take long for her to earn the nickname 'Freebie Fergie'; as Princess Michael, another who saw the wisdom of borrowing clothes, earned the title 'Princess Pushy' before her.

Diana's situation was different. When she married Charles she had a fairly substantial trust fund from which she had income, and she also had the proceeds from the sale of her Colherne Court flat. And that was over £100,000 in 1981. As the wife of the Heir Presumptive she must not be seen to have to scrimp and save, and anything she wanted was provided either by her wealthy mother or her wealthy husband whose income from his Duchy of Cornwall estates is over £1 million a year.

It would have been considered very bad form for her to be seen accepting freebie gifts in the form of clothing, jewellery or holidays. And, her husband already had two substantial homes, a collection of antiques and pictures that would outshine most, and was quite able to afford a full staff to look after her every wish – even if he did occasionally grumble that he couldn't afford it.

At least Diana had early warning of her future husband's attitude to money. Like other girlfriends before her, when she first went to Highgrove she caught him on one of his economy drives. This meant, as his mother had always taught, that no food must be wasted. She found herself eating scraps, tarted up to look more appetising than they were. She discovered for herself that his fridge was often full of food that would have been better thrown away, but was hoarded because it might be needed. He also had the habit of taking a look in the fridge to make sure that the food bought with his money wasn't disappearing too quickly. He once complained that he seemed to be paying for an awful lot of chickens.

'Ah, but you do so like your vol-au-vents, Sir,' the chef said blithely.

Another warning for Diana could have been the sight of a little silver gadget (inscribed with the Prince of Wales Feathers) that rolls up his tube of Maclean's toothpaste, making sure he doesn't miss the last squeeze. It's his valet's job to roll it up!

Actually, Royalty tend to think money is rather vulgar but certainly not to be splashed around. They rarely buy anything new when they have something old that will do. Children's clothes (pre-Diana) were a perfect example. She changed all that. Before her, the same Royal prams lasted for generations and were hauled out of the Buckingham Palace attics whenever a new baby came along. And the Duchess of York, who is by nature more in the Royal mould when it comes to money, will probably do things the way the Queen has always done them. She is less likely than Diana to see anything wrong in the habit of handing things down.

But apart from a dislike of spending money, the truth is that Royalty have little real knowledge of the stuff. The only time most of them ever use or even see cash itself is in church.

The Queen always puts £5 into the collection, and even this is handed to her by her Equerry in an envelope so that she does not actually touch or see it. It comes with her prayer book, ribbons carefully placed in the correct pages for the service by the Equerry.

The late Stephen Barry, who was valet to Prince Charles for twelve years, told how for many years his Sunday morning job was to leave out £1 for Prince Charles to put into the collection plate. Prince Philip continually told his son that this was not enough until the Saturday evening when Barry found a note asking him to leave out £5 ready for church parade the next day. Underneath Charles' signature was scrawled the word 'Inflation!'

In the morning, Prince Charles picked up the £5 note from his dressing table, stared at it wonderingly and asked what it was. He gave every impression, said Barry, that it was the first one he had ever seen.

The Prince is fascinated by the conception of self-made wealth. Indeed his Prince's Jubilee Trust charity works to set up young people in their own businesses. After attending a reception in the States once where every guest was mega-rich, he remarked, 'The wealth in this room could probably pay off our National Debt.'

It did not seem to occur to him that his mother's wealth could probably do exactly the same thing. The Queen's revenues from the Duchy of Lancaster work out at about £1.5 million a year (untaxed). The Treasury bill for the Civil List in 1989 was £6,195,300 – cheaper than expected because the Queen refunded the Civil List allowances paid to the Gloucesters, the Kents and Princess Alexandra out of

90

her own funds. But it is the hidden costs that put up the bills: £10 million to refit Britannia and £40 million for new aircraft for the Queen's Flight, both paid for from the Defence Budget. Then there is the upkeep of Royal Palaces, paid for by the Department of the Environment, and contributions to foreign tours, paid for by the Foreign and Commonwealth office. Palace post, incidentally, goes free. The cost of maintaining the Crown is about £80 million a year. Cheap at the price, many would say.

Their money is carefully nurtured. Edward VII put the Royal finances on the straight and narrow with Cassels, the brilliant financier who advised him. The Civil List money is paid in one lump to the Queen and it is promptly put on short-term loan. She pays her relatives bit by bit through the year – like wages, which is what the Civil List is, in fact.

But with the exception of the Queen Mother, all the senior royals strive not to appear to be rich. They do not behave like Arab sheiks – not only because they do not wish to, but also because they feel that any signs of ostentation would irritate and offend. And the lesser members of the family simply haven't the money anyway to be seen to be extravagant.

There was an occasion when Prince Charles' Aston Martin had to be serviced and a Rolls Royce was sent as a temporary replacement. When the Prince came downstairs and saw the limousine, he was furious.

'What's this?' he demanded to know.

When told it was the replacement car, since there wasn't anything else available, he reluctantly drove it. But he grumbled that being seen in such an expensive car was bad for his image.

But apart from their favourite 'fun' cars, such as Charles' £80,000 Aston Martin, a gift from the Amir of Bahrain, the Royal Family have their cars on an advantageous leasing agreement. Thus Prince Charles had a Turbo Bentley for a while and Princess Anne has just acquired the latest model for herself, complete with calf-upholstered seats and a specially sprayed exterior.

'If Charles can have one, so can I,' she was heard to declare and instructed her private secretary to telephone Rolls Royce and arrange for her to borrow one for a few days to see if she liked it. She obviously did, as she is now the proud owner (well, leaseholder) of a £90,000 Turbo Bentley.

Apart from the Queen, the family like fast, sleek cars. Before he married, Prince Charles once dreamed dreams of treating himself to a Rolls Royce Corniche. One Easter when his parents were away he was staying with his grandmother at Royal Lodge rather than disrupting Windsor Castle for one visitor. He asked for a demonstration model of the Corniche to be brought to Royal Lodge at Windsor, intending to try it out after lunch.

The Queen Mother arrived back at her home from church ahead of the Prince to find this magnificent car sitting in front of her elegant house, looking like a picture from Country Life.

Mr Terry, the man who then looked after the Royal Family's cars, was leaning on the bonnet but he immediately straightened up and bowed as the Queen Mother came towards him.

'Good morning, Mr Terry,' she said, inclining her head towards the car. 'And what is this?'

Mr Terry explained it was a sports Rolls Royce which he had brought along at Prince Charles' request. The Queen Mother walked slowly around the car and commented that it was really very fine.

Mr Terry applauded her judgement and then asked diffidently if she would like to try it out?

Never one to turn down a novel experience, the Queen Mother graciously nodded and waited for the door to be opened for her.

When the door was opened, Mr Terry leaned inside and began to tip the front seat forward so that Her Majesty could climb into the back. It was probably the first time in her life that she had ever been faced with a two-door car. She looked a touch puzzled, and then taking a step backwards, murmured, 'Perhaps another time, Mr Terry. Another time. . . .'

Prince Charles never did buy the car for fear of appearing extravagant, and the Queen Mother, of course, has a perfectly good Daimler or two of her own.

The Queen Mother, who started life as a daughter of an earl, has always, like Princess Diana, been a happy spender. She gives the most generous parties and she not only shamelessly indulges others, but whenever she feels like it, she indulges herself. Her table is by far the grandest of all Royal households with lobster, champagne and asparagus out of season. She thoroughly enjoys the good things of life and shares them with her friends and family. There is no austerity at either Clarence House in The Mall or Royal Lodge in Great Windsor Park. At one time she had a chef who was somewhat to the Left in his views. His face would register total disapproval as she gave him her menus for the day. And when she had finished her list, she would smile winningly at him and say, 'It's only a little treat.'

When she was eighty she spent £100,000 renovating the kitchens and dining room at Birkhall, her home on the Balmoral Estate.

Those in the know believe that she did this as she intends to leave the house to her favourite grandson – Prince Charles. And Charles loves Birkhall, preferring it to Balmoral because, he says, it is 'so cosy'and the Prince likes things that are cosy.

Travel is a fact of Royal life. They are always having what might be termed 'business trips' and not unnaturally they are reasonably cheerful at landing an 'out of town-er' to somewhere warm and sunny when it is cold and wet here. There is also the possibility of saving money when off on an official engagement. Princess Margaret was always ready to volunteer to give any Caribbean Island its independence. As someone said sourly: 'Heaven knows what's she going to do for tickets once they've given away the Caribbean.' But Princess Margaret is not a spendthrift, and any job that gives her a lift in the general direction of Mustique where she has a home is a bonus.

None of them is above such tactics. If the Prince wants to play polo in some other country, he'll fix himself an official trip to cut down on the fares.

Sometimes this isn't all that easy. When, in 1983, Princess Anne's husband was going to Australia on equestrian business she wanted to go with him. But the first-class fare to Australia (as Princesses do not travel club, let alone tourist), is formidable. Anne let it be known that she would be available to go on a Royal tour at that time, if Australia would like her to come.

Unfortunately, Australia said not at the moment. They would pencil her in for a few year's time. Anne, however, fixed it by agreeing to do a television interview in Australia, providing the television company paid her fares.

This was not really a snub to the Princess because the Prince and Princess of Wales had been there only the year before. More important probably to the host country, a Royal tour costs a great deal. Having a Royal visit is fun for the host country, but it is a costly business. And it is the host state who pay – fares, accommodation, everything. If the tour is a long one, the staff will change in mid-term – meaning double fares. It does not cost the Royal Family a penny. Even their wardrobes are paid for by the Foreign Office and that is the extent of the British financial involvement in an overseas tour.

On a much smaller scale, the Royal Family just visiting a private home can become expensive. Extra servants always have to be hired and a small household can be stretched. Royals may relish such matters as the Order of the Bath but they do expect to have to clean one.

It is something of a puzzle to know why saving money is of such importance to the Queen and Prince Charles. Neither has ever been short of funds. Maybe they inherited the trait from Queen Victoria whose worst fault was her meanness. Prince Philip is penny-pinching, too, but that is more understandable since he has never had any money of his own. His parents, exiled from Greece, were penniless and dependent on handouts and accommodation from better off relatives and rich Royalists, also exiled, who supported them – providing roofs, holidays and paying the young Philip's school fees. Philip's father, Prince Andrew of Greece, was an extravagant man with expensive tastes. He ended his days living with a wealthy widow, Madame Andrée de le Bigne, on her yacht in Monte Carlo, while his wife, Philip's mother, devoted herself to a religious order and lived in spartan simplicity.

Philip's father was also an accomplished free-loader, which Prince Philip most certainly is not. All his married life he has sung for his supper. But when he married the young Princess Elizabeth all he had was £6.10s in the bank, and his pay as a Royal Navy lieutenant was £11 week. Marriage would boost this by the married man's allowance of £4.7s.6d. His worldly goods just about filled two suitcases. Therefore, in the beginning, he was entirely supported by his wife and the British taxpayer.

To such a macho man, this support was perhaps difficult to come to terms with and explains why even today he works so hard to make the Queen's Estates into paying propositions. He is forever trying to cut back on the cost of running the Royal homes. He was particularly keen on this in the early days of the Queen's reign. He was also desperately anxious to modernise the Palace, make it more efficient and drag everyone screaming into the twentieth century. The Queen, recognising that he needed something positive to do, let him get on with it. It was a time when her husband, having been forced to abandon his career in the Royal Navy when she became Queen, was restless and unhappy. Chaffing against the Royal cage, he escaped from it by long trips abroad as often as he could. At home, he was a whirlwind of reforming activity. It is possible that the Queen, who dislikes change, might have felt that reorganising the Palace would keep him at home for a while.

Eventually, Prince Philip brought in a tycoon of public industry, Sir Basil Smallpiece, to reorganise the running of the Palace. The very thought of a time and motion study put both Palace Staff and Officials into a panic. Sir Basil's men were going to clock everyone's daily routine and no one's daily routine was hectic enough to bear much scrutiny.

Among the most worried men was one of the Duke's Pages. It is true that when Prince Philip, always obsessed with travel, is on one of his rare visits to London his staff are worked off their feet and exhausted by the time he flies off again. He crammed in twice as many engagements as anyone else into half the time. But when he is away, which is often, there is nothing for his staff to do. They grumble that they hardly ever see their master.

The Duke's Page was aware that if his master was away when the time and motion study men called, his role in the running of the Palace was not going to look too significant.

Then he had a stroke of luck. He learned that the Duke would be home for an entire week. He took himself off to the time study men and suggested that might be the best time for them to follow him around then.

They fell for it.

When their report was returned to the Palace after weeks of painstaking work, it contained one particular recommendation. And that was that the Duke's Page really could do with some extra help!

It is not just this generation of Royals who count the pennies. A favourite remark of Queen Victoria, when asked for financial help by any one of her relatives, was that 'pearls do not grow on bushes at Windsor'. But perhaps the most money-conscious Royal ever was the Queen's grandmother, Queen Mary, whose childhood was blighted by lack of it. Her mother, Mary Adelaide, granddaughter of George III, and daughter of the Duke of Cambridge, was pretty of face but enormously fat and the Royal Family despaired of ever marrying her off. Nevertheless, rather late in life she ensnared and married the dashing and handsome young German, Prince Francis of Teck.

He was four years younger than his bride and penniless. And he jumped at the chance of marrying into the British Royal Family.

Queen Victoria gave this odd couple a grace and favour apartment in Kensington Palace where they lived and entertained lavishly with no prospect whatsoever of paying the bills. History repeats itself. Princess Michael of Kent, also living in a grace and favour apartment at Kensington Palace, has similar difficulties, and she, like the Tecks before her, has had to sell off some of the family treasures, her butler carting it, discreetly wrapped, to Christie's, the auctioneers. At least Marie Christine, as the family call her, tries to supplement her income by writing books. Queen Mary's parents were constantly in debt perhaps because it was Mary Adelaide's contention that the British should support their Royals.

Unfortunately the British did not comply. And, unlike our present Queen who is generous towards her relatives and frequently bails them out, Queen Victoria did not comply either.

From the age of seven, the future Queen Mary was aware of the endless procession of tradesmen presenting their accounts. There was never money to pay for anything. The debts eventually became so disgraceful that when Mary (or Princess May, as she was called) was sixteen, the Tecks were bailed out by the resentful Cambridge family and exiled to Florence where life was cheaper. The grace and favour apartment was taken back and all their household possessions sold at public auction.

It was a humiliation that the future Queen of England never forgot. The problems that the lack of money brought to her family so dominated her thoughts that she was never able to shake off the nightmare fear of being poor again.

Her money consciousness took a curious form. She was a great lover of antiques and beautiful things, though not particularly knowledgeable about their value. Her great passion was royal memorabilia. She was an assiduous collector, and wise hostesses hid anything that might catch her eye when she visited their homes. Queen Mary was apt to pressurise to be given whatever took her fancy and if all else failed, to help herself.

She spent the war years at Badminton House, the Gloucestershire home of the Duchess of Beaufort. When peace came she returned to London and one or two things belonging to the Duchess of Beaufort came with her. Among them was a silver kettle which rested on silver gates.

The Duchess of Beaufort said nothing at the time. But after Queen Mary died, the Duchess asked the Queen Mother if she had come across a silver kettle which rested on silver gates. The Queen Mother said she hadn't seen it, but if she ever did, she would let the Duchess have it back.

Actually, the Queen Mother saw it every morning. The kettle was in constant use on her breakfast tray. No doubt she thought the Duchess was talking about some other kettle entirely.

There are off-beat little perks which come the Royal Family's way, such as using the Army as beaters when they go shooting. The official explanation for this is that it gives the soldiers some exercise. It is also a lot cheaper than paying thirty men for a day's work out on the moors.

'Unto everyone that hath shall be given' is particularly applicable in the case of the Royal Family. They receive a lot of presents. The basic rules are that presents should not be accepted, except under special circumstances, like weddings, christenings and State visits. Before her marriage, Princess Diana was bitterly disappointed when a famous firm offered to give her the jewellery she wore for a series of special photographs. Royal rules decreed, however, that she had to send it all back.

'But I'm not Royal yet,' she protested.

The rules about accepting gifts seem to be bent, though, occasionally, and at times, it seems, it is acceptable to keep one if no one finds out. Charles and Diana gratefully accepted £1,200 worth of baby furniture from a shop in North London, but sent it back when the donors talked about it.

There were no problems about keeping wedding presents. The most spectacular of these were a matching bracelet, watch, earrings and necklace, made with whopping great sapphires and set in gold. They were a gift from the late King Faisal of Saudi Arabia.

'Gosh,' Diana said in tones of deepest awe. 'I'm becoming a rich lady.'

Princess Margaret had similar luck when at much the same age as Diana she was given a box of diamonds which were made into an exquisite necklace. They were a gift from the South African people and presented to her by Field Marshal Smutts during a tour of South Africa. The Queen has a magnificent emerald set – a gift from the President and people of Brazil on her Coronation day. And Prince Charles did very well when the Emir of Bahrain presented him with his £80,000 Aston Martin.

Another Arab potentate gave him a pair of gold cufflinks, worth about £1,000, but they are never used and are still knocking about in a drawer somewhere. Why doesn't he wear them? Charles thinks that they are too flash, too glitzy.

Good fortune does smile on them. Diana experienced this eagerness that people have to give to Royalty on her Caribbean break in January of 1988. Tycoon Richard Branson lent her and her party of fifteen (including her mother, sisters and children, plus nannies, detectives and chief lady-in-waiting, Anne Beckwith-Smith), his island, Necker Island, complete with a ten-bedroomed mansion.

The house and island normally rent out at £4,200 a day but that does include fridges bursting with champagne and caviare, all meals and drinks, a jacuzzi, a fresh-water swimming pool and all manner of speedboats and sailing craft.

The Princess and her party stayed for a week on the island which Branson hoped would provide her with a private holiday away from prying eyes.

Other members of the family, too, have been given substantial gifts that they have managed to hold on to. Prince and Princess Michael of Kent were given a plot of land in Antigua by Peter de Savary. Princess Alexandra had a house in Sardinia given to her by the Aga Khan and, of course, Princess Margaret still has her house, Les Jolies Eaux, in Mustique, built on land given to her as a wedding present by her long-time friend, Lord Glenconner. These gifts have a two-pronged effect. They please the recipient and add a great deal of prestige to the donor. Richard Branson will never have to worry about letting his house for almost £5,000 a day. Princess Margaret put Mustique on the map, and she too lets her house for substantial sums; and Princess Michael and her husband helped make the St James' Club on Antigua the fashionable spot it is today.

It is not always big things that arrive gratis. Anything from new novels from the publisher to gifts of after-shave from the manufacturer arrive unsolicited. Valets and dressers are forever being sent things by shops and companies, hoping that the Royals might be persuaded to use them as a step towards a coveted Royal Warrant for the company concerned.

Sometimes these items are sent back, but much of what arrives goes 'into stock' to be recycled and given as presents to someone else. 'That can go away for Christmas,' Charles has been heard to say when something arrives that he doesn't want to use and cannot be bothered to send back. Otherwise, the valet or dresser is told they can keep it if they like. Someone once sent Prince Charles an after-shave with a sporting name. He smelt it suspiciously, recoiled and said he didn't want it. It landed up with one of the footmen who thought it smelt rather good though the rest of the Palace inhabitants were not so sure.

Prince Philip was once sent after-shave which he didn't want either. Joe Pearce, his valet, kept it and slapped it on one morning before going to wake his master.

The Duke's first words of the day were, 'What's that bloody smell?' Joe, thinking it might be the drains, opened the windows wide before going for his master's breakfast.

'I can't understand it,' said the Duke when the breakfast trolley was wheeled in. 'That smell gets worse.'

'I can't smell anything, Sir?' Joe volunteered. 'Well, I can,' snapped the Duke. Puzzled, the valet retreated to the pantry where another member of Staff was working.

'He's complaining about a smell,' he said, 'but I can't smell anything.'

'Could it be your after-shave?' his colleague asked. The valet had rather overdone it.

'Oh, my God!' Pearce said, realisation dawning, and rushed to scrub it off. It must have been that, too, because the testy Prince Philip stopped complaining.

The Palace cellars are stuffed with household equipment and furniture, some of it antiques belonging to the family, but mostly gifts from foreign tours, weddings, christenings, all kept tucked away in the hope that they might come in useful sometime. And they do. The Queen opens up these Aladdin's caves whenever members of her family marry, to help them set up home.

When Princess Diana married, one of her presents was a particularly fine kitchen from a German manufacturer. The press discovered this and sounded off, asking what was wrong with British kitchens. Surely, the argument went, the heir to the Throne should have a British kitchen in his home?

This was all a bit embarrassing since in fact Highgrove does have a good British kitchen – also a wedding present – and the German kitchen had been installed in a staff cottage in the grounds that is lived in by Ken Stronach, the Prince's valet.

The Palace had a problem. They could hardly admit publicly that the German kitchen had been relegated to staff quarters. And the staff themselves had a bit of fun ringing up Mrs Ken Stronach, pretending to be the German firm, and saying they wanted their kitchen back!

Some presents are an embarrassment. While in power, Madame Imelda Marcos of the Philippines sent the Prince of Wales a mass of picture albums – of herself. She also sent him a boat. When he got word that it had arrived unexpectedly at Windsor Mews, the Prince, keen to see what sort of craft it was, took himself off to have a look.

It turned out to be a huge twin-engined speedboat. But unfortunately there were no engines. Checking on the price of these, he got the answer that they were £18,000 and the boat needed two. No way would Prince Charles spend £36,000 on something he didn't need or even particularly want. He had a brilliant idea. He gave the boat to a youth organisation and the Queen's Jubilee Appeal paid for the engines.

Being given presents is all very well, but the Royal Family do resent people making money out of them. The Emanuels, who made Princess Diana's wedding dress, fell foul of this for a while. They found themselves the recipients of too much publicity and became famous in the process.

'We'll see about them,' said the Princess.

The Emanuels' thoughtful wedding present was a white leather album containing photos of the birth of the dress – pictures of themselves with the sketches, the seamstresses working on the dress and finally the finished dress itself. The album also included photographs of their premises showing how the windows had been covered to defeat prying eyes.

Flipping through the album, Princess Diana asked, 'How can we get these silly pictures out and use the book for something else?'

There are those in the family who cry poverty. Princess Michael is one, but then she genuinely is a have-not. By Royal standards the Michaels are hard-up. Second sons of Dukes are not eligible for the Civil List, and Prince Michael is a second son. He must live on what he earns or, hopefully, inherits.

The late Duke of Gloucester was one to cry poverty, too, and over the years the Queen gave her uncle a financial helping hand. Like the Michaels of Kent, the Gloucesters aren't wealthy by Royal standards – at the wedding of the King of Nepal the present Duchess had to iron her own dress – but the present Dowager Duchess, Princess Alice, was the third daughter of the seventh Duke of Buccleuch, Scotland's largest private landowner. But, she still asked if the gardener could have the pot back when she presented some of her staff with pots of chyrsanthemums for their Christmas presents one year.

There are times when they unwittingly become the guardians of our money. During the summer months when the court is at Balmoral, repairs are attended to in the London Royal residences. One year the linoleum in the staff corridors at Clarence House was found to be worn and the Queen Mother pointed this out to a man from the Department of the Environment. He suggested that it might be better to replace the lino with carpet tiles.

But on being told how much this would cost, the Queen Mother thought for a moment and shook her head. 'No, I don't think so,' she finally said. 'I know they like their lino.'

So, lino it was. Though in fact the cost would not have affected the Queen Mother, as the Department of the Environment are in charge of Royal homes and pick up the bill.

The late Lord Mountbatten also cried poverty. The drawing-room carpet was threadbare and in order to raise some much needed cash he opened Broadlands, his Hampshire home, to the public. He had hoped to draw the crowds by saying that this was where the Queen and Prince Philip had slept on their honeymoon.

In fact, the first days of the wedding had not been a happy time for the newly-weds. They were plagued by both photographers and public, driving Prince Philip into a frenzy at this foretaste

100

of his future. Elizabeth lost a treasured little gold watch when she was walking in the grounds of the house. It has never been found and the older staff find themselves kicking through leaves, still looking for it forty-one years later.

At Broadlands whenever she had visited her Great Uncle Dickie, the Queen always slept in a four-poster in the pretty Victoria and Albert pattern chintz which decorated Portico Room. This room has a bathroom en suite and its own little private Chinese sitting-room. Visitors to the house were shown the rooms and told 'the Queen sleeps there' and it was always let slip that she had been there last week or even yesterday. A little door was added to ease the tourist queue and enable visitors to have a good look at where the Monarch lays her head.

At first the venture was not a success. Broadlands is not Blenheim or Woburn and once Lord Mountbatten opened the house, the Queen was not too keen to visit. She had enormous affection and respect for her Uncle, but she was well aware that he twisted situations to his own advantage. He was trying to use her for his own ends, and she cannot be seen to be involved in commercial ventures.

It took endless telephone calls and letters before Lord Mountbatten persuaded her into taking her Saturday ride in the grounds – while the public were there. Eventually, to please him, she capitulated. After her first visit she agreed the alterations were very nicely done, and that she didn't mind the extra door in her room. But she said, 'Nevertheless, one knows they [the public] are there. It's just like mice scurrying along.' The possibility of seeing the Queen out riding produced a lot more mice to scurry. The attendance figures dramatically improved.

Lord Mountbatten had managed to convince himself that poverty was about to fly in through the Georgian windows of his gracious home, and he also managed to convince his friends of the same thing.

One of his closest friends, the novelist Barbara Cartland worried about his finances and was always giving him 'treats' and making sure he wanted for nothing. She showed him enormous generosity.

She was not unnaturally hurt and surprised when after his tragic death, it was discovered that he had left a considerable fortune.

# At Their Majesties' Pleasure

It would be impossible to write about those things that give members of the Royal Family great pleasure without mentioning the Queen's corgis. All the Royal Family are dog people even Princess Diana, though she doesn't care for them in the house. Princess Michael is the only Royal who is crazy about cats but she breeds yellow labradors as well. The Queen herself breeds both corgis and black labradors. She also owns them for her own personal pleasure.

Those who know her well believe that her dogs give her the chance to show affection in a way that she cannot often do with human beings. And she does adore them. She fusses over them, pets and pats them and lets them sit on her lap. They are her pampered babies and she feeds them herself, mixing the food in their bowls, sometimes down on her knees using a silver spoon and taking the food from a silver tray carried by a footman.

When it comes to Royalty, being born with a silver spoon in the mouth applies to the corgis as well.

They don't get tinned food, either. The kitchens supply the dogs' food and liver is favourite. Tough, old stags shot at Balmoral are beheaded, drawn and cleaned and sent down on the Royal train to the Palace. There they are jointed and cut in 3lb portions and stored in the deep-freeze as dinner for the Royal dogs.

All the Queen's private rooms have a special corner where the bowls are set down. The dogs stretch out under the table whenever the Queen is eating, waiting for the moment when every now and again she feeds them breadsticks. Yet they don't fuss for food; they are too fat and lazy in spite of being well-exercised, either by the Queen's footman or the Queen herself. They all sleep together in one room, known as the Dogs' Room, which was once used by the Queen's ladies-in-waiting. Each dog has it's own tartan rug, and there is an extra heater in the room in case the temperature falls.

When the Queen makes her weekend visit to Windsor where her corgis are bred, one of the first things she will do is make a foray to the kennels to see the new arrivals. As soon as the puppies are old enough to leave their mother, Her Majesty usually takes one back to the Palace to join the group that are always at her heels. If there's a 'mistake' that is often the one she will pick. The other corgis are given to people who she knows will provide a good home. She likes to know how they are getting on and will often recognise the dog before she recognises the person to whom she gave it. Over the years there have been hundreds of corgis and finding kennel names for all of them can be quite a problem.

The Queen has a novel way of solving this. She chooses new names for puppies from the obituary column in the *Times*. When he was younger, Prince Edward used to help. The system produces off-beat ideas and it is interesting to consider how many Top People live on having given their distinguished name to a Royal corgi.

The dogs are almost as important to the Palace staff as they are to the Queen. They act as an early-warning system. The staff always know when the Queen is near from the pattering of twenty-four (at last count) paws, and the clicking of the Queen's fingers as she encourages them to follow her. They cause little trouble. It is not true that they bite – and they are beautifully house-trained. What is true, and curious, is that the dogs know the minute the Queen gets into the lift on the ground floor to come up to her own rooms on the first floor. They immediately set off down the corridor and are waiting for her when her Page opens the lift door to let her out.

Bobo and the corgis wake the Queen every morning. The footman takes them for a walk first thing in the Palace grounds and brings them back just before the Queen gets what she calls 'her calling tray'. This is an early-morning cuppa and biscuits brought in by Bobo along with the dogs. Bobo opens the curtains, Prince Philip drinks the tea and the dogs take the biscuits.

All the Queen's corgis are raised by Mrs Fenwick, a pleasant woman who runs the kennels at Windsor. Mrs Fenwick always telephones when a new litter is born. She is one of the few who can ring through to the Queen at any time – even in the sacred dinner period when instructions are that the Queen is not to be disturbed by phone calls. Mrs Fenwick looks after the dogs whenever the Queen is abroad or on the Royal Yacht. There is no question of them going to boarding kennels – they become part of the Fenwick household, a real home away from home since Mrs Fenwick is as besotted with dogs as the Queen.

The Queen houses the Fenwick family in a Gothic house that looks like a small castle on the Home Park at Windsor. Mr Fenwick is Head Gamekeeper for the Windsor Estate. He has to share his house with dogs, dogs and more dogs, and it is said he is always sweeping them off the furniture, but in a surreptitious way so as not to upset either his wife or Her Majesty.

When the corgis die, they are buried in the grounds at Sandringham. The Palace carpenter makes a proper wooden coffin, the gardeners dig a hole, the Page orders a posy and the dog is laid to rest with a simple little ceremony. Eventually a small headstone is erected.

There is no actual dog cemetery. The little graves were originally just along one of the garden walls. Now they are in pretty and peaceful spots chosen by the Queen herself.

During their lives they are much-travelled animals, equally at home on land or air. They are forever on and off aircraft. They never go on the Royal Yacht – the Queen worries about them falling overboard and they would certainly not be taken overseas as quarantine applies to them, as for any dog. When the Queen is overseas they are comfortable on Mrs Fenwick's sofas. The Royal train, too, is a second home to them. They travel on it to Balmoral and whenever the train carries the Queen on her engagements. She herself puts down newspaper on her compartment's beige carpets – in case of accidents. And when she sleeps the night aboard the train, early birds sometimes spot the Queen's footman out alongside the railway line, the dogs yapping at his heels, as he gives them their first run of the day.

It is helpful if Her Majesty's footmen like dogs since there are so many of them about. At one time the Queen employed a footman who was highly popular with her – partly because he was so popular with the dogs. Whenever he came into the room the corgis would make a bee-line for him, jumping up to greet him and barking excitedly.

'You're so good with the dogs,' the Queen would say, and he would mutter modestly that, yes, they did seem to like him. One day another member of the staff persuaded him to reveal his secret. It was really quite simple. The footman always kept a lamb chop in the pocket of his tailcoat!

Labradors are another of the Queen's loves and she gets pleasure from training those she breeds herself as gun-dogs. The training of all the gun-dogs on the Royal estates is supervised by the Queen and her idea of a really splendid afternoon is to spend it on the moors with a shooting party, well behind the guns, working the dogs and picking up shot birds. This is hard and tiring work, but she does have incredible stamina.

Her sister, Princess Margaret, thinks all this trudging about is crazy and has always thought so. Even as a teenager her description of a shooting party was 'popping of horrid guns at silly birds!' But then, she is less of a dog person than her mother and sister. She did once have a King Charles spaniel called Rollie, but her dresser looked after it most of the time. It was also an accident prone dog, always doing things like falling on railway lines. But it survived to die a natural death.

For a while, just after he married, Prince Charles decided to give up shooting and gave his guns to Prince Andrew. Princess Diana had a strong hand in this decision. The Queen was horrified. She prefers to take a low profile when it comes to blood sports, being well aware that the wholesale slaughter of birds holds no favour with some of her subjects, but even so, pheasant and grouse shooting are very much part of Royal Family life.

As much as she loves Prince Charles, she is reputed to have said grimly, 'He had better take it up again, if he wants to stay part of this family.'

Her reaction was strong because the sports that the Royals pursue provide employment for a great many people. Should there be a general falling off in popularity – and the Prince of Wales' views on any subject are liable to influence others – the Queen was concerned that many people would be left without work. Prince Andrew is not a country person nor particularly sporty. Who would lead the shoot in days to come if Prince Charles opted out? And she was upset that he had given away his superb guns. They had belonged to her father, King George VI, and were insured for more than £20,000.

The Prince's defection and Princess Diana's victory proved to be short-lived. Charles is now back shooting and, when his wife permits, takes his sons with him.

For many years Prince Charles had a labrador called Harvey who was bred by his mother. Harvey was a particularly fine dog and after he was shown at Crufts he made a small fortune at stud. The only trouble with Harvey was that he was never properly house-trained. Prince Charles used to say ruefully that the dog had soiled some of the finest carpets in Britain. Princess Diana was not enamoured of poor old Harvey and did not appreciate his fondness for carpets. He was relegated to a kennel in the inner courtyard of Kensington Palace and much to his chagrin, one outside at Highgrove, too. It was a dog's life after what he had been used to – travelling with his master and accompanying him on long fishing trips. After developing arthritis in his back legs, a common complaint for labradors and retrievers, he was looked after by Graham Newbold, Charles' former chef, who gave him a basket in the downstairs staff quarters. Finally, even climbing the stairs became too much and the Comptroller of the Household, Lieutenant-Colonel Philip Creassey, took him to his country home in Kent as a family pet.

Since 1986 Prince Charles has had an adored Jack Russell called Tigger, who accompanies him almost everywhere. Tigger was a gift from Lady Sailsbury, a family friend, and caused a bitter quarrel between Charles and Diana over the question of his tail.

Diana was horrified when Charles suggested docking Tigger's tail. She felt it was cruel and pointless to do it as it would normally have been done when the puppy was a few weeks' old.

'The two stormed away, arguing furiously,' a member of the staff recalls. 'It became the subject of local gossip for a long time, but Diana won. Tigger still has his tail.'

The Duchess of York is also a fan of Jack Russell terriers and her father, Major Ronald Ferguson, has one called Bella. It was Fergie's fondness for the breed that prompted Andrew to buy her a puppy to keep her company during the last few months of her pregnancy while he was away at sea. Bendicks, a tiny black and tan puppy, arrived and was seldom out of her sight. Fortunately he has adapted well to Princess Beatrice as the breed are not noted for their gentleness with babies.

The Queen has her own unique breed – Dorgis – as well as Corgis. These are the result of a romantic meeting between Princess Margaret's long-haired dachshund, Pipkin, and one of the Queen's corgis. The only current member of the Dorgi clan is Piper. Smokey, Shadow, Spark, Myth, Fable, Diamond and Kelpie are typical of the imaginative pet names the Queen's dogs are given.

The Princess Royal was the recipient of one of the corgi puppies, Apollo. Son of the Queen's corgi, Spark, he is a great favourite with the children and is seldom happier than when he is down a rabbit hole. He lives contentedly at Gatcombe Park with Random, a Dumfriesshire hound cast-off from the local hunt.

It was the Queen Mother who sparked the family interest in Pembrokeshire corgis. There were always a couple of them about the house when the Queen was a girl. When her father became King, two called Jane and Dookie moved into Buckingham Palace with the rest of the family. Today the Queen Mother still has two. She always has two and apparently a pair that have now died were rather talented. One night when their mistress was going to a musical evening at St James' Palace she went through what is known as the door-in-the-wall – an adjoining door between St James' Palace and Clarence House. The woman organising the evening waited to greet the Queen Mother and dropped a deep curtsey, which revealed to her Royal guest that she was wearing a magnificent tiara. The Queen Mother was bare-headed. Flustered enough at what appeared to be a bit of blatant upstaging, the woman then spotted that behind Her Majesty pattered her two corgis.

'Oh, Your Majesty,' the woman said, presumably to draw attention away from her headgear. 'The dogs!'

'They'll be all right,' the Queen Mother said, smiling sweetly. 'They're very musical, you know.'

Like her daughter, the Queen Mother also enjoys a shooting party. When she is hostess at one of her own at Birkhall, her home on the Balmoral estate, instead of giving lunch in the open she likes to put up the huge tent which her late husband always used when he went shooting. It is enormous, almost big enough to double for the Big Top and, being made of canvas, it is extremely heavy. But the Queen Mother will never part with it or buy something more manageable because it belonged to the King.

Her staff fight to get it up using poles and pegs and ropes, none of which is particularly effective if the day is at all windy and more often than not it is at Balmoral. One solution is to hold the tent in place by Landrovers parked on the corners pinning the canvas down with their wheels and weight.

Her luncheon guests, enjoying River Dee salmon and straw-berries with cream from the Queen's home farm at Windsor, served by footmen from silver trays, might be alarmed to know that outside, the staff and policemen are desperately attempting to prevent the tent from blowing away.

Those who know the Queen well say she would have been perfectly content to have lived in the shires breeding dogs and horses. Away from Buckingham Palace this is the life she seeks. At Windsor and Sandringham, she is up first thing in the morning, and down to the Royal stables where the groom already has a horse saddled up for her ride.

It is an old passion. When she was a child, living at 146 Piccadilly before her father became King, on cold mornings when her breath made clouds in the air she would sigh with pleasure and say, 'Just like a real horse.' In the house itself she and Princess Margaret had a stable of thirty toy horses. They stood on the top landing arranged under a dome in the roof. Each wheeled horse stood a foot high. Every night Elizabeth and her sister 'fed and watered' these horses and carefully removed their saddles and bridles and put them back again in the morning. It was an obsession that lasted until they had real horses of their own. And as a child Elizabeth talked of making a law that there would be no riding on Sundays so that horses could have a rest too. She also wanted to decree that no one must ever again dock a pony's tail.

She has a passion for racing which sometimes impinges when she is out with the guns. If there is a race meeting where her horses are running she likes to know how they are doing. But she can't be on the moors and at the racecourse. So, while she trudges through the heather, her chauffeur sits in her Landrover listening to the radio. As the results come through, he stands on the vehicle's roof, making energetic tick-tack type signs to the Queen to let her know if her horse won or lost. And back at the Palace, one of her Pages will video the television so that she can watch the afternoon's racing at her leisure. So great is her interest she even has the French racing papers delivered to her every day.

The best possible day out – even better than a day on the moors – is spent at the races, particularly if one of her own horses wins. The Queen Mother feels much the same, except that her favourite meeting is Cheltenham where her own steeplechasers have a good record of wins. As we have mentioned, she doesn't like to sell her horses, so some time ago she began giving Prince Charles the yearlings that didn't come up to scratch to use as hunters. The Queen breeds his polo ponies at Sandringham for him and these contributions help him to indulge in these two very expensive sports – which are two of *his* favourite activities.

All the Royal Family are horsey people – again with the exception of Princess Diana. A childhood riding fall which broke her arm put her off horses for good.

'The whole business of riding scares the life out of me,' Diana admits. 'I lost my nerve following the accident years ago.'

To please both her husband and the Queen she has made valiant efforts to overcome her fear, but for her, sitting on the back of a horse is no great pleasure.

Prince Charles himself came late to his love of horses. When he was younger he felt rather the same way about them as his wife does. But once he took up hunting he began to ride with enthusiasm. His sons now both have their own ponies, Trigger and Smokey. The children's ponies are kept in the stable yard at Highgrove and are looked after by groom Marian Cox who taught the boys to ride. William loves going bareback through the long grass no doubt pretending, as Princess Anne did before him, to be a Red Indian. This scares the life out of Diana who frets like mad when she sees her boys having riding lessons. She need not worry. Marian Cox is an excellent teacher, and during the summer months takes William and Harry to local gymkhanas where they are entered under the names Master William and Master Harry Cox.

The young Charles was not so brave. He called his first pony William as years later he was to call his first born William. He was fond of the animal, but not too keen to ride him. He very much liked visiting the mews at Windsor and feeding William with an apple, but he rarely spent more than fifteen minutes a day on his back.

Princess Anne had no pony of her own at that time and was always cadging rides on William and had to be dragged screaming from the saddle. Today her prowess as a horsewoman is legendary, but even when she was almost too small to ride, the grooms at the Castle used to say that she would make a fine horsewoman. So, eventually William became more the property of Anne. William was a docile fellow but like all ponies inclined to stumble on unfamiliar ground. He did just that when Princess Anne was riding him one day. It was the first of the many tumbles she has since taken. Her attitude then was no different. She flew over the pony's head and was back on her feet before the accompanying groom could pick her up, her bottom lip quivering dangerously.

'Don't cry!' the groom said. 'There's no point in crying.'

'I am not crying,' Anne said defiantly. 'But William should not have done that! He really should not have.' Then she climbed back on again and set off at a sharp trot.

Prince Philip is proud of his daughter and accepts that she is a more skilled rider than he has ever been; though he, too, was very good. Polo was his passion, and a rough, tough player he was, giving his ponies a hard time. But severe arthritis in his hands ended that. He took up carriage driving instead. To everyone's surprise

Prince Michael took it up as well, and he and the Duke can be seen competing at the same events. Princess Michael is another horsey Royal, determinedly so – perhaps in an attempt to fit in better with her prickly relatives. She hunts with the Beaufort (where Prince Charles hunts) and surprisingly, she took up dressage at the age of thirty-nine after her second child was born. She went into it truly seriously engaging the top English equestrienne, Pammy Siveright, to teach her as well as taking private lessons at the Talland School of Equitation near her Gloucestershire home. It did look suspiciously as if she were trying to outdo Princess Anne, but as it happened Princess Anne, at the age of thirty-four, was giving up competitive riding just at the time Princess Michael began. But there were some raised eyebrows when it was announced that Princess Michael's latest endeavour was learning to ride side-saddle which she did with great promise. The Queen is the only member of the Royal Family who does this. And even then, the only time she ever used the skill was in the days when she conducted the Trooping the Colour ceremony on horseback.

It is true to say that most of the immediate   Royal Family all enjoy the same things. One could call Prince Andrew a professional photographer since his interest in the camera is so great. And, of course, much of his work has been published and exhibited. But probably the keenest photographer in the family is the Queen. Among her prized possessions are the family albums which she has built up over the years – all with photographs she has taken herself.

She has a small, gold-plated camera that was a present to her many years ago, and with this she has chronicled her children's lives. She may be the world's most photographed woman, but she enjoys taking pictures herself, and, indeed, is rather good at it. The albums show year by year the life of her family; lots of pictures of the corgis, a small Prince Charles with his first cricket bat and with his first set of gardening tools (a present from his granny when he was five), and certainly by now pictures of William and Harry.

The Queen puts in all the album pictures herself, usually when she is in her private sitting room at either Sandringham or Balmoral. She writes little comments underneath to remind her of the occasion – just like any other proud mother.

These photograph albums travel wherever she goes. They are packed up by her Page and taken to all her holiday homes. The only time she leaves them at home is when she goes on a State visit to a foreign country.

Prince Charles, too, is a keen photographer, but his vast collection of pictures, snapped all over the world, are not kept in albums. They are carefully filed by his valet, labelled and kept in drawers. He has hundreds and hundreds of them, and once they are developed and put away, he never seems to look at them again. In recent years his interest in the camera has waned. He now prefers to paint his favourite views rather than photograph them. He leaves the camera to Diana who by her own admission is not amazingly good, but enjoys snapping away.

The masses of photographs that the Royal Family take have always been processed by Wallace Heaton of New Bond Street, who have four Royal Warrants, one from the Queen, the others from Prince Charles, the Duke of Edinburgh and the Queen Mother, respectively. Their films are developed by one trusted employee and kept under lock and key, marked top secret. Wallace Heaton have never let the Royals down, but there have been two occasions when pictures have got away. The first time was in 1964 when *Paris Match* published a picture of the Queen sitting up in bed, holding the newborn Prince Edward, and surrounded by her other children. The Queen was outraged, but it was never discovered who had purloined the picture.

Prince Charles was furious when some rather blurred and obviously snatched photographs of him and Diana on their honeymoon were published. They had been taken aboard Britannia although the crew had been told that no one was to bring a camera on to the ship. Someone did, it was never discovered who.

Then in 1988 to the Palace's fury, a photograph of the Duchess of York with her new baby Beatrice, the Queen and the Queen Mother appeared on the front page of the *Sun* newspaper. The picture had been sold to the newspaper for £1000 without the Queen's permission. But what made her crosser was that she had planned to use it for her Christmas card that year. Linda Heggarty, the seventeen year old who had helped herself to the picture, panicked when she read that the Queen had personally ordered a major investigation, headed by the head of Scotland Yard's serious crime squad. Linda went to Scotland Yard and confessed.

She had been opening mail at her £86-a-week job at the International Masters Publishers when she spotted a big white envelope with Balmoral stamped all over it. Inside was the picture with a letter from the Queen's secretary saying that Her Majesty wanted the picture printed as this year's Christmas card.

The girl took it to her bosses who were puzzled because the company only prints books about house plants.

'For a lark,' said the girl, 'I rang up a newspaper and when they offered me £1000, nearly a quarter of my year's salary, I was so pleased.'

The Queen was not. And so, printing the picture cost the *Sun* £100,000, split between four charities of which the Queen is patron. And such is the power of the Monarch; Linda's own family wouldn't speak to her when they discovered what she had done.

It was entirely the Queen's decision as to whether Linda should be prosecuted. She was not.

When he is not charging about a polo field, Prince Charles' pleasures are mostly quiet and contemplative ones. He used to enjoy cooking. In the days when he was up at Cambridge he would get himself over to Wood Farm on the Sandringham Estate and cook, though his ability was no greater than grilling steaks and making bread and butter pudding. Everyone had to eat vast quantities of the stuff.

The Klosters avalanche disaster in which his close friend Major Hugh Lindsay was killed, has not diminished his love of ski-ing and for him the enjoyment is as much in the surroundings as in the ski-ing itself.

'The Prince of Wales loves the mountains,' says his friend and ski guide Bruno Sprecher. 'They give him a chance to enjoy peace and solitude which is not easy when you are so famous that everybody knows your face. Sometimes we would ski off into the middle of nowhere and he would look so happy. There was time to trace deer tracks in the snow, gaze at the beauty of a frozen waterfall or look up at an eagle soaring overhead.'

Many of the Princes's pastimes are nature oriented. He paints water-colour landscapes of his favourite places. He gardens. The Queen Mother began to teach him about gardening when he was five years old and it stuck. He enjoys getting his hands in the earth and growing things. Those early leanings and a child-sized set of garden tools have grown into a real interest. When he speaks sharply to the farmers of Britain, he does actually know what he is talking about and he keeps a weather eye on his Duchy of Cornwall tenants since he is a believer in organic farming. The Prince was 'green' long before it was fashionable.

It was back in 1987 when he spent a few days working with a crofter on the Hebridean Island of Berneray. Dressed in overalls he tended sheep, planted potatoes and built dry-stone walls. Charles was taken secretly to the remote Scottish island by his cousin, Lord Granville, and delighted the locals by working alongside them and joining in a sing-song at a traditional local party. Yet some newspapers branded him a hermit and the headline in one ran 'A Loon Again'.

The Prince wanted to taste the crofter's life but some of his critics seemed to think a desire to do this meant that the Prince of Wales was going mad. One might say it was a better thing for our future King to do with his spare time than the lifestyle of the last heir. That Prince of Wales, who happily was never crowned King, preferred to sail around the Mediterranean on a borrowed yacht and in the company of someone else's wife.

Our Prince would rather go fishing – something else his grandmother taught him. It is an abiding pleasure for him as it was for her. Even at eighty the Queen Mother was still standing in thigh-high freezing Scottish waters, a fishing rod in her hand. A favourite fishing place for both was a particular stretch of the River Dee which runs through the Queen Mother's Birkhall Estate.

For her eightieth birthday, the Royal Family, so well aware of her love for Scotland and the outdoor life, clubbed together to buy her a fishing hut on the Dee.

The hut – which does not have electricity, but does have a proper lavatory – is four miles from her Balmoral home, Birkhall. It looks like a log cabin with a pretty front porch set with bench seats, and the family could not have given a present that would have pleased her more.

A hut it may be called, but it is big enough for giving the parties that she so enjoys. Sometimes she has a quiet dinner there, though it will be a full production for the staff with silver, hot plates and hot food from Birkhall. The night will be lit by hurricane lamps and a fire will be burning to give extra light and warmth on a chilly Scottish summer evening.

Of all the Royal Family, it does seem that it is the oldest member who has the most fun. The Queen Mother is almost ninety but she still has a busy diary of engagements. When one of her longest-serving staff suggested perhaps it was time he retired, she replied, 'Why? I haven't.'

Her staff stay and stay and even though she is tougher than we think, and they still adore her. She herself likes to be domesticated and since she gets up at 7.00a.m. in the morning but doesn't appear until 11.00a.m., she often makes her own bed so that everything looks tidy.

Above all, she loves people. The Queen's idea of bliss is a quiet and peaceful lunch on her own. The Queen Mother's idea of bliss is a crowd for lunch, someone popping in for tea and out with a party for dinner and a show.

She never eats alone. Her Household are always invited to take lunch with her, whereas the Queen's and Prince Charles' Households always have their meals separately.

Most things please the Queen Mother. She gives herself what she describes as little treats and one of these is a simple television dinner for two, preferably shared with one of her grandchildren. She loves watching the television. Her footman places the set near her big red wing chair. Card tables are set up facing it, covered with white linen and beautiful china and glass along with two straight-backed, dining chairs (the Queen Mother's with arms). Then while Her Majesty watches the box, dinner is formally served! Standards are not dropped. If there are three or more for dinner, the meal is served in the nearby dining room. And viewing has to wait awhile.

The habit of dining in front of the television began when Prince Charles was younger. Charles and his grandmother would settle themselves at about 8.30p.m. to enjoy their supper and the show at the same time. Now that Prince Charles is married, she still has her TV suppers, but usually with Princess Margaret for company since the Princess herself is so often alone.

She has always enjoyed food, and one of her joys is a new box of chocolates. She only likes the soft-centred ones, and she dips into the box, takes an experimental bite, and if the chocolate turns out to have a hard centre, she pops it on the mantelpiece as a little treat for the corgis. As she does not like to give the dogs too many chocolates and then only one at a time, it might have to stay there for a while. Often a collection grows. This is good news for the corgis but not for the housemaids who are never quite sure whether they should throw them away or not.

The Queen Mother and Princess Margaret are the only two Royals who really enjoy a drink. Princess Margaret likes a Scotch, and one of the Queen Mother's favourites is champagne. On a long flight in one of the Royal aircraft she is always served dry Martinis. For many years they were mixed for her by Air Commodore Archie Winskill, who was Captain of the Queen's Flight.

When he retired and mixed his last jug for her, she drank a toast to him and said contentedly, 'Archie, you mix the best Martini in the air and William (her Clarence House steward) makes the best Martini on the ground.'

But then the Queen Mother has never been lacking in a sense of adventure. Right up until the age of eighty-eight she was a great traveller, toddling off somewhere every year, either borrowing the Royal Yacht Britannia, which she loves, or taking an aircraft of the Queen's Flight. She jumped in and out of helicopters like the rest of us jump on and off buses. At the beginning of 1989 her Private Secretary, Sir Martin Gilliatt, announced that she would be slowing down a little. For a lady as old as the century she was certainly entitled to feel the time had come to take it a bit easier.

Even nowadays, her idea of fun is rushing about the countryside in her big American Ford estate car. She is always driven, but she is not one to tell her chauffuer to take his time. The car is one of those that seems to stretch a block, with a back window that winds down to pour in dogs, children and picnic baskets. She has had the car since the mid-seventies, and though she does not use it in London she keeps it garaged at Clarence House along with the more sedate Daimler. The Ford is driven to Balmoral or Sandringham when holiday times come.

On her Windsor weekends she uses the Daimler and she also has a remarkably fine Jaguar, which she is not so keen on because she prefers big cars with lots of leg room. Prince Charles used to love it when he was younger. It has a horse motif on the front which appears to be galloping as the car goes along. It has been known to make bad travellers feel quite queasy.

The Queen Mother is not one to get queasy. Even in the country she always sits in the right-hand back seat behind the driver. About the only thing she ever does that shows her age is to have a little nap in the car on a long journey. In the Daimler, there are blackout screens, and she'll pull them down and doze gently, particularly in the heavy London traffic on a Friday afternoon when she is on her way to Royal Lodge at Windsor.

None of her enthusiasms has waned except fishing which she has reluctantly given up. She is handy with a billiards cue and likes a quiet flutter on the horses – if she wins the money goes to charity – and is an avid reader of *The Sporting Life*.

As a child she once wrote in a school-friend's autograph book that the thing she liked doing best in the world was making friends. And she has been doing just that for all her life.

Both her daughters are good mimics and they inherited that from her. Ever since Princess Margaret was a child, playing the Principal Boy in Windsor Castle Christmas pantomimes, she has adored anything to do with theatricals. She was sufficiently talented to have become a showbusiness professional had she wanted to, but at the time that was unthinkable. It seemed pretty unthinkable for Prince Edward, too, but he has managed to get away with it, working as he does for Andrew Lloyd Webber's Really Useful Theatre Company.

Princess Margaret longed to go on the stage, but it was not to be. Another disappointment among many. She had compensated by becoming the Royal Family's most knowledgeable theatre-goer. She sings well and is a talented pianist. Songs from the shows are her speciality. In her younger days some of her closest friends were theatrical personalities, like Danny Kaye, whom she adored, and Peter Sellers, who was also a close friend.

As a stunningly pretty young girl she made an appearance at a fancy dress party at the American Ambassador's home in Regent's Park. Those who saw it will never forget it. She appeared as Madame Fi-Fi, wearing a can-can outfit, complete with black panties, stockings and suspenders. She performed the can-can and finished by throwing up her petticoats and wriggling her bottom at the audience. But there were those among the Royal Family's advisers who thought Princess Margaret had really gone too far.

But of course when you are a princess or a duchess there is always someone anxious to say you are going too far.

There were frowns after Diana and Fergie's little escapade at Annabel's and more frowns over Diana's wild dancing with the young bachelor Philip Dunne. It is true that both young ladies had a lot of fun, playing about at the Derby, quaffing champagne at Ascot and pushing each other about in the snow at Klosters. But when the public criticism became rather sharp they cooled their antics and began working at a more serious image. Mercifully, however, neither is likely to lose their sense of fun.

'Contrary to public opinion,' said Diana in a speech, 'I am not about to become an alcoholic.' This form of public confrontation is a trick the Princess has learned from Prince Charles, who livens up his speeches by quoting some of the more unlikely things that the media have criticised him for.

Diana is not an alcoholic and there is no danger of her becoming one. She hardly drinks at all. Her pleasures are far more simple. The Princess enjoys dancing, which she does at least twice a week for exercise, and she enjoys swimming every day in the Buckingham Palace pool. She also plays the piano (her grandmother Lady Fermoy was a concert pianist).

Entertaining friends she finds great fun, and as Charles is so busy she has learned to do this without him if necessary. Small dinner parties are arranged and afterwards everyone plays bridge or watches a film. Forays into nightclubs are rare and if she goes to a restaurant it is usually at lunchtime.

San Lorenzo in Chelsea is a favourite and so is Morton's in Berkeley Square. Recently under new management this one-time hideout of second-hand car dealers has been spruced up. Diana has a corner table away from too many prying eyes and her favourite lunchtime dish is fishcakes. In San Lorenzo she usually tucks into a plate of pasta. On the day in February 1989 when Prince Charles flew off to Washington to meet the new President, the Princess of Wales was lunching with one of the Queen's Equerry's at Green's oyster bar in Mayfair and astonished fellow customers with her appetite. She drank two glasses of Sancerre, and ate crab salad followed by a mixed grill. This consisted of kidneys, liver, sausage, filet steak, a pork chop and mashed potatoes. And after that there was apple crumble. A mere 1750 calories! Contrary to the public's impression, the Princess enjoys her food.

When she is in the country the Princess likes to take long walks in nearby Badminton Park or stay at home doing needlepoint. Like her husband she is fond of gardening and has become quite expert on wholesome organic cuisine. Tennis and swimming occupy most of her free time in the summer months. When she is not feeling all that energetic, Diana finds pleasure in photography and has all the latest equipment, including a video camera to monitor the rapid growth and antics of her two lively boys.

Fergie is also a fan of photography. Her husband is almost professional in his ability and, always anxious to share in his hobbies, she too has become quite proficient. She is also determined that Andrew will enjoy her interests and drags him off to the ski slopes whenever possible. Andrew is nowhere near as good on skis as his daredevil wife – an experience he finds rather humiliating.

As he neither drinks nor smokes, he finds social gatherings a bit of a bore and is not nearly as accomplished at cocktail chatter or even public speaking as Fergie. At dinner parties, which they give whenever possible in their temporary home, Castlewood House on the edge of Great Windsor Park, Fergie is the gracious hostess making sure everyone has drinks and feels at ease. Andrew, preferring one to one conversations, is inclined to single out a guest and almost pin him or her down in his anxiety to discuss something serious.

Despite his social awkwardness Andrew and Fergie have a very loving relationship and enjoy things together. In particular they like discussing plans and ideas for their new house, which is being built in Sunninghill Park, with their interior designer Nina Campbell.

The Duchess has learned to pilot both fixed-wing planes and

helicopters and has recently mentioned that she would like to take up flying jets. She also has parachuting in mind.

She often complains she cannot find enough hours in the day and it is hardly surprising; she is a mother, a Duchess with many Royal duties to perform and a Navy wife who tries to give Prince Andrew her undivided attention when he comes home

Now there is her latest venture – she is an author. Her two children's books are both about a helicopter called Budgie. Showing the enthusiasm she has for so many things, Sarah went all out to publicise the books and help their sales. All the profits will go to charity.

'Fun?' she says. 'I don't have time for that,' and then adds with a laugh, 'I try to make everything fun and give whatever project I am involved with all the enthusiasm I have.'

And that cannot surely be a bad way to try to live one's royal life.

# Travelling Royally

One thing about being royal is that if you are late for the plane you do not have to worry. As Prince Charles once said to an agitated aide who was anxiously watching the clock, 'Keep calm, don't worry. They won't go without me.'

The Royal Family are among the world's most seasoned travellers. With the exception of Russia and her satellites, there are few countries in the world that the Queen, Prince Philip and Prince Charles have not visited at some time or another. As Prince Charles says: 'I'm just a roving Ambassador for Britain', and he and his relatives are remarkably successful at it. A State visit from the Royal Family creates friendship and if tension is there, it can certainly be eased. But they also drum up trade for Britain.

One of Prince Charles's first tours took him to Japan and while he was there the Sony management mentioned to him that they were thinking of building a factory in Europe.

Immediately he said: 'Why don't you build it in Wales? There's a perfect place near Bridgend.'

To his delight, the Japanese took up the idea. The second phase of the factory was opened by Princess Diana in 1982, and now the Sony works is well established and providing valuable jobs in a depressed area of Britain.

The Queen is not allowed by protocol to indicate which countries she likes the best, but Prince Charles has made no secret of his pleasure in visiting both Australia and North America.

It is possible, though, that the Monarch does share her son's preferences as she rarely misses an opportunity to travel to either of those two continents. For Royalty, visiting Australia and Canada is rather like home. The Australians and Canadians are always pleased to see them, but rather take them for granted – like members of the family. So, if they make the odd mistake, nobody takes much notice.

In the United States there are hazards. Democratic Americans have been known to ask the kind of questions which make the Queen's accompanying officials turn purple. But after a lifetime of upholding the dignity of the Monarchy the Queen is rarely left without an answer. And sometimes one suspects she is really enjoying herself and entering into the spirit of the occasion.

In February of 1983 when the Royal Yacht Britannia sailed into San Diego harbour for a visit to the USA, the weather was terrible, with pouring rain and high seas. As the Queen is said to suffer from seasickness, this must have made her journey something of an ordeal.

But she was as composed as ever at a party to meet her rain-soaked American guests from newspapers, radio and television. One television commentator asked her if she would be riding when she arrived at the President's ranch.

'Of course,' said the Queen. 'That's the whole purpose of the trip, isn't it?' He then asked her what she and Prince Philip would be doing on their visit to the Yosemite Valley in Northern California.

'Staying at an hotel for the weekend,' she informed him. 'It will give me a chance to put my feet up for a bit.'

The commentator broke the off-the-record rule that applies when meeting the Queen at one of her own parties. He reported the conversation to his viewers that evening.

The protective British officials were outraged that the Queen should have been quoted, but the Queen herself finds such anxieties tiresomely overblown. And, understandably, she gets quite irritated when her most ordinary, simple everyday remarks are reported as if she had said something of world-shattering significance.

But it is true that she rarely expresses an opinion about her position. In the United States on that occasion she nearly did. When the film *The Prince and the Pauper* was mentioned, she was asked if she would like to change places with the pauper. According to the reporter her reaction was that she would not like to be a pauper and that she found being the Queen quite pleasant enough, thank you.

But normally protocol rules. No opinions expressed and no emotions shown. As the Duke and Duchess of York, the Queen Mother and her husband went to Australia. While they were away, King George V wrote giving them their instructions on how to behave once they arrived home where the family would be waiting to greet them at the quayside. The Duke was permitted to take his hat off, but he must not kiss his Mama, Queen Mary, while in public. Sometimes now the Royal Family do exchange a public peck on the cheek, but it is still a rare sight.

It is amusing how countries who have got rid of their monarchies are so fascinated by ours. France is as hungry for information about our Royal Family as we are ourselves. America, so staunchly republic, has great curiosity about Royalty. One of the things that this land of excesses is particularly fascinated by is the Queen's jewellery. They want to know if it is all real. When assured that there is not a brilliant in the entire collection, even the richest American finds it hard to believe that the Queen has no costume jewellery at all and that every glittering chunk is strictly kosher.

Prince Charles loves the USA. He is impressed by the energy and the friendliness of the American people and fascinated by the country's wealth and size. Though he normally moans and groans about overseas trips (he really does not like to stay anywhere longer than three days, except at Balmoral or Sandringham), an invitation to the USA is accepted with alacrity.

The first time Prince Charles went to Washington was in 1970 and President Nixon was in power. The President made a determined attempt at match-making the Prince with his daughter Patricia. He could just see her pretty head on a stamp as the next Queen of England.

Both Patricia and the Prince seemed equally appalled at the prospect!

The next time he went to America, it was 1977. Jimmy Carter was in power. 'At least I won't have a daughter to face this time,' he said before he left.

He did, though, have to face being chased by the girls. He was mobbed by groups of drum majorettes, all intent on a kiss. 'God,' he said once, looking out of a plane window and seeing about thirty girls waiting to greet him, 'they'll smother me!'

His eight visits to the USA as a bachelor were all open-season, but on his ninth visit he took a wife along for protection. Pre-Diana, Australia was equally hazardous. There he was ambushed on beaches by ambitious young ladies determined to get both a kiss and their pictures in the newspapers. With the appearance of Lady Diana, all that stopped.

Before Prince Charles and Diana married, she had never been to the USA and the Prince was anxious to take her there. She was keen to go, but the Royal Family normally must have a specific reason for a trip. The Prince could not just whisk Princess Diana off in Concorde so they could both enjoy a weekend's sightseeing. Although less important Royals like Princess Michael flit off to the States all the time, usually using a different name if they wish to be incognito.

If the Queen or, in this case, the heir to the throne is keen to visit a country they have to subtly let it be known that they would like to call as invited guests. Which, of course, from their point of view is a great deal cheaper even if rather more long-winded. Charles and Diana's trip in November 1985 all went through the usual diplomatic channels with the Foreign Office in London first informing the British Ambassador in Washington that they (the Waleses) would be interested in coming if they (the host country) would be interested in having them.

Royalty cannot invite themselves.

As it happened, the USA was very interested in the Prince and Princess making a visit. Everyone there wanted to get a look at Diana.

An invitation was therefore officially offered, and accepted, for a date in the future. The excuse for the trip was to visit the President and his lady at the White House while a British trade week was going on in Washington, and also to raise money in Florida for United World Colleges, Prince Charles' pet charity.

From then on the preparations took months. Early in the year the visit was discussed during what is called the Spring programme planning meeting. This is a conference where the Prince and his officials begin to sort out exactly what he will be doing over the next year. All requests for him to attend a lunch, speak at a dinner, open a new building, unveil a plaque, make a personal appearance for charity, visit a hospital or make an overseas visit are considered at either this meeting or another held later in the year. Each individual's engagements have to be dove-tailed in with the rest of the family.

An important factor in the planning of official visits is that traditionally a Royal guest must always be greeted by the Lord Lieutenant of the county they are visiting. There was once a near disaster when two Royals arrived at different ends of the same large county on the same day.

The Royal Family are all dog lovers including Princess Diana who is
holding a small admirer during a visit to Dartmouth. Her stunning
outfit is by her favourite designer, Catherine Walker, and the hat by
milliner, Philip Somerville. *(Alpha)*

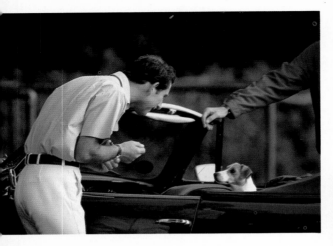

*Below* At Sandringham there is a special doggy burial ground in a pleasant spot under the trees. The head stone above belongs to the Queen's special favourite, Susan, from whom most of the rest are descended. *(Alpha)*

*Above* Prince Charles and his Jack Russell, Tigger, who has place of honour in the back of his Aston Martin, appear to be discussing the day's polo. *(Glenn Harvey Collection)*

*Below* Guarding the stairs at Balmoral is one of the Queen's many corgies. The wallpaper dates from the time of Victoria and is embossed with her cypher. There are plenty of spare rolls so it can be replaced when necessary. *(Alpha)*

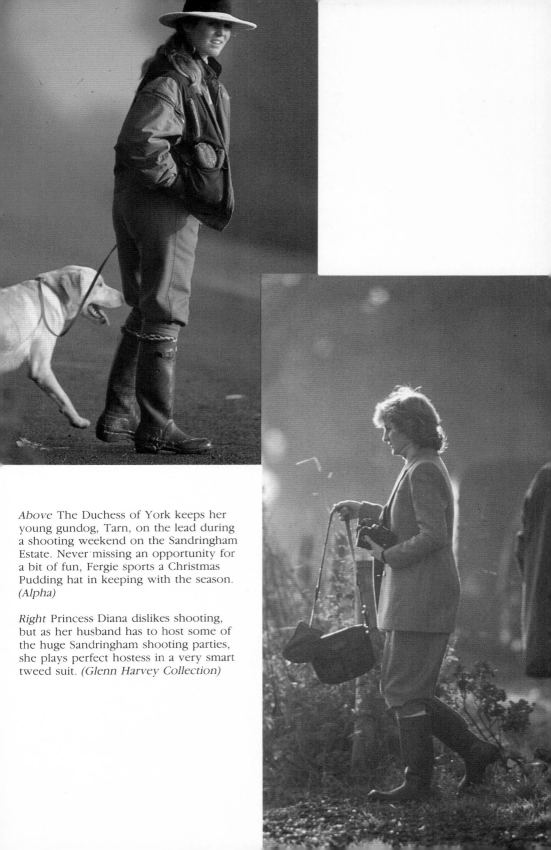

*Above* The Duchess of York keeps her young gundog, Tarn, on the lead during a shooting weekend on the Sandringham Estate. Never missing an opportunity for a bit of fun, Fergie sports a Christmas Pudding hat in keeping with the season. *(Alpha)*

*Right* Princess Diana dislikes shooting, but as her husband has to host some of the huge Sandringham shooting parties, she plays perfect hostess in a very smart tweed suit. *(Glenn Harvey Collection)*

*Left* The Queen feeling most relaxed in a headscarf unflatteringly gripped to her head and a camera in her hand. If you look carefully you can just see her cypher, EIIR on the top of the Leica. *(Alpha)*

*Above* Prince Philip's current passion is carriage driving and he competes in shows all over Europe, often driving the Queen's team of fell ponies. Here he is at Windsor Horse Show, which he uses as an opportunity for him to entertain some of his many German relations. *(Alpha)*

*Left* Playing polo from a bike is not as easy as Prince Philip makes it appear. He was forced to give the game up several years ago because of painful arthritis in his wrists. *(Alpha)*

Work combined with the greatest pleasure of all for mother and daughter — horse racing. Here the Queen and the Queen Mother enjoy a day at the Epsom Derby. In spite of owning and breeding many horses, Derby victory still eludes the Queen. *(Alpha)*

*Right* Prince and Princess
Michael of Kent waltz to the
Blue Danube during a
Viennese evening. The
beautiful Princess has great
style and here she wears a
beaded ball gown by
Gianfranco Ferre. *(Alpha)*

*Below* Prince Charles
enjoying the best of
Hollywood during his
bachelor years. He is standing
between Sophia Loren and
Farrah Fawcett-Majors, who
he thought very attractive,
but was surprised at how
short she was. *(Alpha)*

*Above* Prince Edward and television presenter, Selina Scott take part in a charity clay pigeon shoot organized by former world champion motor racing driver, Jackie Stewart. *(Glenn Harvey Collection)*

*Right* Prince Charles at the controls of a helicopter. Both he and Prince Philip love to fly and take the pilot's seat whenever possible. *(Glenn Harvey Collection)*

*Below* The first female member of the Royal Family to learn to fly both a fixed wing plane and a helicopter, the Duchess of York adjusts her helmet for a test flight with the Red Devils acrobatic team. *(Glenn Harvey Collection)*

*Right* The Queen Mother with three generations of her family on the quayside at Scrabater during the annual cruise of the Western Isles *(Glenn Harvey Collection)*

*Below* Having reached Balmoral, the Queen delights in having as many of her family around her as possible. Here she is with Prince Philip in the sitting room of their highland home with one of the corgi and daschund crosses — the dorgi, at their feet. *(Alpha)*

*Right* Princess Margaret and Prince Edward in the Royal barge tender to Britannia which transports family and guests from the magnificent yacht to the mainland to have lunch with the Queen Mother at the Castle of Mey. *(Glenn Harvey Collection)*

Happily such mistakes are rare. Each member of the family has his or her own planning meeting, including Princess Diana since not all her engagements are in the company of her husband. Anyone wanting to nobble a member of the Royal Family for an appearance at any occasion would be well advised to write at least a year in advance. And even then be prepared for a polite refusal. The Foreign Office lays a claim to their time as well, wanting members of the family to undertake goodwill visits and be present at independence ceremonies and State weddings, overseas. There are discussions as to which member of the family should be allocated which particular job. When Zimbabwe was given independence, it was decided that since there was a guerilla war raging in the country, it would not be wise for the Queen to go. The task was delegated to Prince Charles. And with Nicholas Soames, one of his favourite people, as his Equerry at the time, it turned out to be a good trip.

Once the dates suggested by the USA for the Washington trip had been finally approved by the Prince and Princess they were written in on the huge board in the Prince's office that plots all their movements. A board, incidentally, that for security reasons is kept well out of the sight of casual observers.

The routine never varies regardless of which country is the host or which member of the family is the guest. Two detectives, the Prince's Private Secretary and one of the Prince's press officers journeyed to both Washington and Florida for what they call a 'recci'. In February 1989 Charles made an identical trip to visit the newly-elected President Bush and then play polo in Florida. A 'recci' is a reconnaissance which looks into accommodation, making sure the rooms are suitable, and other similar checks. In Prince Charles' case, making sure that the bedroom has heavy curtains as he likes to sleep in the pitch dark. Princess Diana, who is a light sleeper, cannot bear a room where there is any noise. Security arrangements are scrutinised and everyone who is to have close contact with the Royal visitor will be briefed down to details such as his or her tastes in food and even the type and size of towels they prefer. This advance guard then comes back to brief the visiting Royal on the background of everyone that he or she is likely to meet.

When the Queen goes abroad this 'recci' is headed by her Travelling Yeoman. It is all immensely thorough and complex. It also works.

A great deal of special preparation goes on in the host country as well. It is always a bit of a nightmare for the British Ambassador in the USA beating his head against a brick wall trying to explain that it is not protocol to call the visitors Liz and Phil or Chuck and Di. That he is Sir and she is Ma'am. That curtseys and bows are in order. The Americans do not want to know. Certainly not about curtseying.

Eventually the Ambassador gave up the unequal struggle. When Princess Diana made her successful official visit to New York on her own in February 1989, it was formally announced that, since the Americans had won their War of Independence, curtseys and bows would not be necessary.

Diana's visit to New York was eagerly awaited and it was a topic that filled many a page in the newspapers. Columnists pondered on the significance of her trip without Charles, who was expected there two weeks later. Amateur psychologists insisted this meant the marriage was not a good one and certainly not the sort of union any red-blooded American woman would want.

On the other hand, feminists applauded Diana's independence, while political columnists suggested the nation refrained from succumbing to Di-Mania. One observed: 'We once revolted against the British and should be ashamed of any pro-Monarchist yearnings.'

'Who are these people anyway?' an NBC-TV newscaster asked. 'They are just like any other family, except more exalted. And they're not even like Donald Trump [a billionaire real estate mogul with a flashy lifestyle]. They're far too humdrum in their tastes.'

True, all true. But the media might just as well have saved their breath. Diana in New York was a smash hit.

Everytime she appeared, she looked wonderful. Thanks to us. On a State visit of this kind, the Foreign Office supply the Royals with a hefty overseas clothes allowance and, in fact, all the staff who travel with them. Everyone gets an amount to spend based on how important they are. Even the valets get a new suit. So do the policemen, but theirs are paid for by Scotland Yard.

It all means that this particular shopping field day is financed by us, the taxpayer. Fortunately for the Exchequer, the Royal men often do not bother with new clothes since they always have at least a dozen suits on the go. On the other hand, if a Royal male thinks his wardrobe is getting a little shabby, it is a suitably economical move to make some replenishments, particularly for the poorer members of the family.

For much of the time on overseas visits the men of the Royal Family wear uniform for most of the official daytime engagements. Prince Charles has 100 or so to choose from, his father slightly more. But uniforms are never worn on visits to the United States. The USA is considered what the Royal valets call a suit-job. Rightly or wrongly they believe that visiting America calls for a wardrobe of 'plain, double-breasted suits'. They suspect that Americans do not care for uniforms, so the braid and brass buttons get aired elsewhere, like Africa.

This clothing allowance is a delight to the Royal ladies, particularly Princess Diana who adores clothes. She has a field day with her allowance. And quite rightly, too. The cameras of the world are on her wherever she goes. Furthermore, she earns her pretty clothes. Overseas tours are hard work.

The Royals must never for one moment look disinterested, even if they are bored to death. It must never show if their feet hurt, and if they have a headache they must keep on smiling.

In the weeks leading up to departure day, back at the Palace, the packing goes on down to the last tube of toothpaste, the honey and the special bran for breakfast, the special pink pills for the tummy, and the family photographs that the Royal Family never travel without.

They always take along a few helpers – in Charles and Diana's case, their own butler, two valets, two dressers, one hairdresser, one lady-in-waiting and assorted detectives, secretaries and private secretaries. It usually works out around twenty extra people, not forgetting about two tons of luggage.

Part of those two tons consists of presents for their hosts, boxes and boxes of them which the staff carefully label so they do not go to the wrong person. The usual gift is a signed photograph – in a silver frame made by Mappin and Webb for anyone important and in a brown leather frame for those lower on the pecking order such as security men. The photographs remain the same, only the value of the frames change. The Queen generally gives her host an engraved silver tray which more often than not has been recycled from the enormous store of such things at Buckingham Palace. As she hands it over she normally murmurs 'It's rather small. I do hope you like it.' And it is indeed, since these gifts are not paid for by the tax-payer. The Royal Family have to buy them with their own money for those people who are suggested by the Ambassador or Government House.

In politician Roy Jenkins' diaries he recalls a visit to Brussels made by Prince Charles. It was in November 1978 when Roy Jenkins was President of the European Commission.

'He gave me a photograph of himself in a rather nice self-deprecating way, saying, "I am told I ought to give you this.

I don't expect you want it, but I hope you won't do the same as Trudeau who immediately stuffed it into a drawer which was crammed full already of ones of most other members of my family."

'So I said I would not do exactly that and gave him a leather-bound copy of Asquith in return, with which he seemed pleased.'

A few years ago both Princes Charles and the Queen Mother went to Canada. Charles gave out an enormous amount of presents from the list provided by Government House. The Queen Mother was shown this list so that there would be no clash of gifts.

'Dear me!' she said. 'He does seem to have given rather a lot of presents.' No doubt aware that she was expected to give the same. 'He'll learn,' she said, and cut her list right down.

All the presents are packed in fibre-glass boxes for the journey. The boxes generally come back to Britain – full of the presents that the Royals themselves receive. Which, it has to be said, are usually a great deal more interesting than a signed photograph or a small silver tray.

It is imperative that valets and dressers get everything right on these trips. They will receive, from the Lord Chamberlain, a list of all functions and suggestions of which jewellery, medals, etc. should be worn at each. It is the job of valets and dressers to make sure that the correct tiara is packed and that every garment is properly accessorised. This is done by working from a list. Every garment is described and numbered, and the suitcase in which it is packed is numbered. This means that if a particular outfit is suddenly needed, it is easy to find among the two tons of luggage.

No one's clothes get more tender loving care than those belonging to a member of the Royal Family. They pay a lot of people to keep them in good order, even down to those in the linen room at Buckingham Palace who sew on buttons and make small repairs. But it is up to the dressers and the valets to spot that the button is missing before the garment is needed.

Before it takes off the first thing, the first thing that Royal men do when they get on a plane is to change into cords and a sweater to stop their suits getting creased, taking care not to stand immediately in front of the window and reveal the Royal underpants. It is also more comfortable on a long journey. Everything possible is done to minimize jet lag. Sleeping times are kept as near to normal and the times of meals are juggled constantly. If the flight was arriving at perhaps eleven at night, instead of lunch and dinner, the travellers would make it just one meal – probably dinner, served as near as possible to the correct dinner time. They eat in a small private dining area of the plane, but if travelling alone, rather than eat in solitary state they will often invite one of their staff to join them. Prince Charles' valet and policemen knew that nothing would ever be the same again when they flew back from the honeymoon. In the past they had always eaten with the Prince. This time they were outside with the crew, while the Prince dined in style with his new bride.

At night, on one of the Queen's flights, dressers and valets literally sleep at their master and mistress's feet. There is not anywhere else to go. The toilet facilities are as luxurious as is possible on a plane but obviously there are no baths. The Royal men will shave with an electric razor while flying so that there is no chance of appearing before the welcoming committee with a nasty little bit of cotton wool covering a razor cut.

Prince Philip and Prince Charles like to pilot themselves. They generally take off and land, leaving the boring bits in the middle to the pilot. Both of them are qualified pilots, permitted to fly jets.

Neither of them is averse to being given a free ride. Armand Hammer, the American oil multi-millionaire who is a great personal friend of Prince Charles, will always send a private jet if the Prince needs one. And very luxurious these jets are too. Charles borrowed one to take a trip from Vancouver to Florida. It was full of marvellous gadgets and toys. He decided to use the telephone to call a friend in London – and couldn't get through. He said in his resigned way, 'That's life! You make a phone call from 30,000 feet and the number's engaged.'

There are times when it is only sensible for Royalty to travel on a commercial flight and it is a mixed blessing for the public to find themselves on a flight where a member of the Royal Family is travelling. Everything runs late since every single piece of luggage is checked and every passenger checked and double checked. Security is intense which makes this undoubtedly the safest, if the slowest, way to travel. The passengers usually get free drinks once the plane is in the air – as an apology for all the waiting. This tends to make for a noisy flight. On one trip to Australia all the passengers were legless by the last lap and cries of 'Good old Charlie' reverberated around the cabin, filtering into the first-class compartment. Charles, who hates being called by his name by anyone except family, was not amused.

When Royalty do travel on a scheduled flight they go on board first and usually take up the seats in the front row. First-class passengers are on their best behaviour for the journey. Even so, the lights go out when royalty wants to nap!

But it is rare for the Royals to travel alongside their subjects. At their disposal are two helicopters, an old Andover and two new BAE 146 jets which cost about £40,000,000 in 1987, and one Royal train consisting of thirteen carriages. Not forgetting the Royal Yacht. This amount of transport may sound plentiful but when all the Royals are busy on engagements it can soon get booked up.

Actually there is no such thing as the royal train – just the thirteen carriages which can be hooked to different locomotives. Therefore it is possible to see two royal trains in two different parts of the country on one day. The largest single amount of carriages – used when the Queen and Prince Philip travel together – is ten. The carriages are painted a distinctive burgundy colour. Overnight stops are often in sidings so they carry their own steps. In 1976 a brand new Royal train replaced the old rolling stock at a cost of £7 million. This came as some relief to the Queen who swore that the old carriages had wooden wheels! These new carriages enable the Royal train to become part of the high-speed trains now used all over the United Kingdom.

The carriages are like moving homes. The Queen's personal salon is decorated in pastel and beige with easy chairs, a coffee table and paintings of trains on the walls. Adjoining it is a bedroom and bathroom. Prince Philip's quarters contain a dining room that will seat up to ten people.

The extra carriages are for the staff and they also contain bedrooms and an office for the members of the Household who travel with the Queen.

There are also plenty of cars for transportation. Housed in the Royal Mews are five Rolls Royce limousines – the most important being a Phantom VI given to the Queen in 1978 by the Society of Motor Manufacturers and Traders. It has a removable outer roof which leaves a transparent inner lining made of plastic. This enables onlookers to have a good gape, both day and night, when the interior is lit by strip fluorescent lighting. All five of these Rolls Royces are State limousines so they carry no number plates. All of them are painted maroon with special brackets on the roof to carry the Royal coat of arms and the personal pennant of the passenger. The oldest of the fleet was built in 1948 and has the classic Mulliner bodywork.

There are also two Austin Princess limousines which are used for official duties. Princess Anne was in one of these when she was almost kidnapped on her way home to Buckingham Palace in 1974. Happily the attempt was foiled.

The Queen's private cars are of a rather more doubtful vintage. She drives an ancient Rover and a Jaguar and when she is in Scotland she borrows one of Philip's Landrovers. He also has a 15cwt van which is powered by electric batteries and because of the limits of its endurance is restricted to a twenty-five mile radius around Buckingham Palace. His marvellous old Lagonda is now in the Royal car museum at Sandringham. All their vintage cars when past service are now kept there. The Jaguar sport saloons which are leased by Charles, Diana, Andrew and Fergie have been converted to use unleaded petrol. So have Prince Edward's Ford Granada and Anne's new Turbo Bentley.

Early in 1989 Buckingham Palace announced that the Queen was converting her fleet of cars to cleaner, lead-free petrol. Some of the newer ones, such as the Jaguars, had already been converted and if Prince Philip had had his way the entire fleet would have been switched a year earlier. The plan was only delayed because a new petrol storage tank was being built in the Royal Mews.

When President Sadat was assassinated in 1982, there was an element of danger about attending his funeral. The Queen and the Duke of Edinburgh were in Australia and the Prince of Wales and his new bride were at Balmoral on the last days of their honeymoon. Prince Charles wanted to represent the United Kingdom at the ceremony. He and the Princess had met President Sadat earlier in their honeymoon and had liked both him and his wife very much. Princess Diana wanted to go too, but the Prince was naturally very anxious about her safety as the assassins had not been caught. He also had to explain to her that at a Muslim funeral her presence could cause diplomatic and religious difficulties.

The Prince, a Naval officer, decided to wear full-dress tropical kit for the funeral because of the fierce heat of Egypt. He had to find out whether or not white tropical kit was suitable.

His office checked with the Foreign Office who checked with the Egyptian Embassy who pronounced it OK. The Prince's orderly in London found the uniform among all the others and when the Prince flew down from Balmoral and boarded a VC10 at London Airport, his clothing was already on board.

Seven other people flew with him. Lord Carrington, the Foreign Secretary and two of his staff, two police-officers and the Prince's private secretary Edward Adeane and his valet. They were to stay at the British Ambassador's residence for one night after arrival and fly back the next day immediately after the funeral.

Cairo was an uneasy city. It was hot, and people had congregated in excited groups. With three former Presidents of the United States present, plus the famous American statesman Henry Kissinger, assorted Heads of State and other Royalty, the Egyptian security arrangements were stretched.

It was decided that not everyone in the Prince's party would actually attend the funeral. The others would wait at the plane, ready for a fast getaway.

By now, everyone was doubting the wisdom of the Prince wearing white. He would stand out in the crowd, a sitting duck for terrorists. The ex-Presidents, Carter, Ford and Nixon and Kissinger were all encased in bullet-proof vests but the Prince of Wales said he couldn't be bothered.

'If it's going to happen, it's going to happen,' he said in his usual fatalistic way.

But there was a moment when the Prince might have regretted spurning a bullet-proof vest.

'There was a group of guards who seemed to be on crowd control standing in front of us,' he said after the funeral was over. 'Quite suddenly they turned round with their guns pointing straight at us. John and Jim [his two policemen] nearly had apoplexy. I suppose it was just a case of bad organisation, but it gave us quite a fright. We weren't sure exactly what they were going to do, and then they just moved on.'

The Prince was almost the last of the foreign dignitaries to leave Cairo. In his typically thoughtful way he stayed behind to speak to Madame Sadat and give her a personal letter from the Princess. It was after five when he reappeared at the airport, still wearing the gleaming uniform. Almost all the other important visitors were by then well and truly on their way back to home and safety.

Prince Charles also attended the funeral of Jomo Kenyatta of Kenya. Sitting in the same row was Idi Amin. The Prince was dismayed to find the dictator there and refused to speak to him or even acknowledge him. But Africa always holds surprises.

On a visit to the Ivory Coast he was staying at the President's guest house and one of the sights he was taken to see was a large lake – full of the President's crocodiles.

They were being given a dinner of live chickens at the time, but there was a sinister atmosphere about the place as if the crocodiles were used to something a great deal more substantial.

'I wonder what else they use that lake for?' he said thoughtfully afterwards. No doubt he was thinking what others were thinking – that the chickens on the menu were for the sake of the visitors.

Official visits have their drawbacks. It is not possible just to go and do a bit of gentle sightseeing. Royalty get shown what it is agreed they shall see – there is no freedom to wander.

In Hong Kong Charles was guest of the Gurkhas. He is their Colonel in Chief. Across in the New Territories he stayed with them at their barracks and joined them for a camp barbeque where he was served snake – and ate it like a man!

In Hong Kong itself, he stayed in the temporary Government House (Government House itself was being renovated), and saw only what he could see from the window. The hotels, embassies and government houses where Royalty stay could easily be described as very glossy prisons.

In this new age of Glasnost, it begins to look as if the Royal Family may at last penetrate the Iron Curtain in their travels. Previously neither would they have wished to go nor would Russia have wished to welcome them. In these changing times Prince Edward has visited Moscow as Patron of National Theatre and when President Gorbachev lunched at Windsor Castle in the Spring of 1989, he issued a formal invitation to Her Majesty, which she accepted.

In 1975, however, the Russians did invite Lord Mountbatten to represent Britain at the thirtieth anniversary of the Victory in Europe. He was a curious choice. As a small boy he had known the Russia of the Czars, spending holidays there as his aunt, the Czarina, was his mother's sister. He was a living reminder of the regime the Russians had rejected and a direct descendant of a Royal Family that the new system had massacred.

He had not been in Russia since 1908 when he was eight years old so he accepted the invitation with alacrity. The visit was to have a double purpose – he aimed to sell the Russians Rolls Royce jet engines while he was there.

Mountbatten might have been Prince Philip's uncle, but he was not Royal and he was not entitled to the magic HRH prefix. So he journeyed to Russia with just his private secretary and none of the back-up that a Royal would enjoy.

The Russians booked him on their national airline, Aeroflot, but not unnaturally he insisted he must go on a British flight in a plane with Rolls Royce engines. Since they were paying for his tickets, they were not prepared to stand for it. Thus thwarted, he reluctantly flew off in a Russian aircraft muttering that it was bit bloody rich to be messed about by a country that his uncle and aunt had once ruled.

When he and John Barratt landed in Moscow, the welcoming

committee explained that they would be staying with the other distinguished visitors in a private guest house above the town.

Mountbatten had already made arrangements to stay in the comfort of the British Embassy. He had no intention of staying anywhere else.

'That is not possible,' said his Russian hosts, adding that they would require at least fourteen days notice before he could be given permission to stay at the Embassy.

'And I,' said Mountbatten, 'will require fourteen days notice if I am to stay at your private apartments.'

This time they gave in.

John Barratt was astounded at how much of Russia Mountbatten remembered. They were taken in convoy with the other distinguished visitors to the Kremlin for a sight-seeing tour. Unfortunately, though Lord Mountbatten had his pass the KGB man accompanying him had lost his. Therefore, neither of them could go in.

While they waited for the embarrassed KGB man to sort things out, Mountbatten pointed out the room that had been his nursery. And he was not allowed inside; he was disappointed that he could not get in to see it again. The nursery that sheltered the baby Czars was now a storeroom and the Russians had lost the key. Mountbatten had forgotten little about the Kremlin. He fascinated the guards with talk of the Czar and Imperial Russia from first-hand experience, giving them a guided tour of the building as it had once been.

At the banquet in honour of the foreign guests the vast table was laden with caviar with ice swans as decoration. Everyone stood until their name was called, only then were they permitted to take their seats while their Russian hosts sat at the head of the table. Lord Mountbatten wasn't upset, John Barratt recalled that he was amused, and that he felt he was 'in for a penny, in for a pound'. But he did say that the Russians had not progressed very far. 'This is just the sort of thing that would have gone on in my Uncle's day,' he said wryly.

Having taken part in the formal celebrations, Mountbatten was given permission by the Russians to visit Leningrad for a holiday, but they kept adding KGB men to his party. And everytime they added one of their men, the British Ambassador insisted on adding one of his. Each side finished up with twelve in attendance.

For the train journey a special carriage, consisting of a single sleeping compartment, a plush drawing-room and an old-fashioned bathroom, had been laid on and the Mayor of Leningrad was waiting to greet him on his arrival with a programme of activities.

But this was not what Lord Mountbatten had in mind.

'I'm sorry,' he said, looking down his nose at the Mayor. 'I have come here on holiday and I insist on doing exactly what I wish to do, and seeing what I wish to see.'

He then proceeded to dictate exactly what he had in mind. The Mayor, not used to such insubordination, was somewhat taken aback, and even more taken aback when Mountbatten sent away the breakfast of caviar, schnapps and smoked fish.

'Sorry,' he said again, 'but I want an English breakfast.'

By this time the Russians had decided they were on a loser. They gave him his own way. He went to see what was left of the Czar's Summer Palace where he had spent his childhood holidays – the Germans destroyed it in the war – and he went to the Kirov Ballet and sat in the same box in which he had sat when he was eight years old. John Barratt recalls that the visit was a battle of wits between the autocratic English Earl and the obdurate Russians. But it went better than could have been expected.

Nothing similar could happen to the Queen if she does decide to visit Moscow. She would certainly stay at the British Embassy and every last detail of her trip would be planned and agreed before she left.

It is hard to imagine even the Russians arguing with the Queen of England and her retinue. But even if they were to try to, they wouldn't stand the slightest chance of winning.

# Dressing The Part

It somehow does not come as a surprise to learn that the Queen always wears a vest. A very fine silk one, of course, but nevertheless a vest.

Unlike Princess Diana and Princess Margaret, clothes don't really interest the Queen. She is not a vain woman. If she were she would have invested in contact lenses years ago. The incongruity of reading-glasses combined with a tiara when she is making a speech never seems to have struck her.

To perform what she and Prince Philip call 'the job', the Queen must have a fabulous wardrobe in brilliant colours so that she can be seen easily. And it is rare to see her wear the same outfit twice. Yet in what she considers her real life she prefers casual clothes.

In Scotland she wears a kilt; in Norfolk, sweater and sensible shoes; and on the Western Isles cruise in Britannia each August she wears trousers. As Lilibet, she most definitely prefers a husky jacket to Her Majesty the Queen's sables and minks.

Like many men, Prince Philip does not take a great deal of notice what his wife is wearing but there was an occasion when he walked through her dressing-room when Ian Thomas, her couturier, was fitting the dress she planned to wear for the Duke and Duchess of York's wedding. It was a particularly pretty outfit – a lavender frock coat with a flurry of pleats showing beneath. He stopped, looked at her and said approvingly: 'That's nice,' and walked out again. She flushed with pleasure as she is wont to do on the occasions when he says something agreeable.

It is Bobo who is the Queen's main influence when it comes to her clothing. Bobo, old as she is, still has an eye for fashion and knows what looks good. She and the Queen work out the wardrobe for special occasions. They get together in the Queen's dressing-room where there is a little round table. When the Queen is dressing, Bobo puts on it a handbag, matching shoes, gloves and tights ready for Her Majesty to wear.

They were deciding on accessories for the lavender dress when Philip again happened by and the two women were having a bit of an argument about which shoes would go best with the outfit. The Queen wanted to wear the black patent somewhat clumpy style that she favours. Bobo felt they were too heavy.

'I don't want to buy anything new,' the Queen insisted.

'You don't have to,' Bobo told her. And retrieved from the cupboard an elegant pair of dove grey court shoes and several pairs of matching gloves.

'But which gloves?' said the Queen. There were three lengths to choose from but none was exactly right. In order to settle the matter, the Queen picked out one pair of gloves, asked for a pair of scissors and then imperiously laid them on the small table.

'Cut them to the right length,' she commanded Ian Thomas. The couturier picked up the beautiful fine suede gloves and, his heart in his mouth in case he got it wrong, carefully cut them to length.

There were three different hats ready to choose from, one with a small brim, another medium, and a broad-brimmed one. The Queen modelled all three for approval and eventually chose the hat with the larger brim.

Bobo burst out laughing and the Queen wanted to know what was so amusing. 'We were hoping you'd choose that one,' Bobo said, 'but we didn't want to influence you.'

The matter of the hat settled, the Queen asked what jewellery should she wear. Bobo firmly decreed pearls.

'And a brooch?' the Queen asked. She always wears a brooch and maybe feels naked without one.

Bobo's face fell. 'Perhaps not a brooch,' she said cautiously.

The Queen needed convincing that both a brooch and pearls would not look right, and eventually a compromise was reached. For the first time ever the Queen was persuaded to wear her pearls with the diamond clasp on one side.

'It's really vulgar, isn't it,' she asked doubtfully, 'to have the clasp showing?'

It was not easy to assure her that it wasn't vulgar at all, but she eventually agreed and the final result was that at Prince Andrew's wedding, Her Majesty looked as elegant as most of us have ever seen her.

When the Queen has grown tired of her beautiful lavender dress, it will be stored away with all her other old clothing. Buckingham Palace cannot but help have the aspect of a museum, so many treasures are stored there. But some of the most fascinating items kept under lock and key in the cupboards and corridors of the huge building are the vast amount of clothing stored there. All the Queen's outfits, going back many years, have been carefully kept, covered in tissue paper and dust sheets. So have most of Queen Mary's clothes. Even those belonging to the late King George VI are still carefully stored. Very little that these three Monarchs ever wore has been thrown or given away. Staff at the Palace grumble that they are running out of space, which indeed, they are.

The Victoria and Albert Museum would dearly love to get their hands on this rich collection which faithfully reflects the fashions of nearly a century, but it is unlikely that, for the moment, they stand any chance. It would require the Queen Mother's permission for George VI's clothing to be exhibited and there is absolutely no possibility that she would ever give this. The Queen herself is known to dislike the thought of personal clothing being used for an exhibition.

The Queen's wedding dress is still in store. As a young bride she stood out against pressure to have it put on show immediately after her wedding in 1947. Winston Churchill backed her decision. An old romantic, he understood perfectly that she felt that the dress was too precious and too personal to be turned into a travelling show. The dress, designed by the late Norman Hartnell and quite superbly embroidered, was not exhibited until many years later. Sadly it is said that today the silk is perishing, perhaps from the weight of the wonderful embroidery.

When the dress was made Norman Hartnell's premises were in a state of siege, so keen was the world's press to get a glimpse of the young Princess' wedding gown. And history repeated itself when the Emanuels were working on Lady Diana's wedding dress. They covered their windows with blinds which were pulled down day and night so that no one could so much as catch a glimpse.

'The press went through our waste-bins, they tried to peer through our windows,' said the Emanuels. 'They waited on the doorstep. Our workrooms and salons had to be lit all the time by electric light, even in the middle of the sunniest day in June.'

Their loyal precautions worked. No one got wind of the beautiful dress.

The Princess has a different attitude from her new relations as to what's to be done with clothes that can't be worn in public anymore. Rather than wear them out or hoard them as her mother-in-law does, Diana gives them to her sisters or her girl friends. At the wedding of one of her close friends, Philip Dunne, early in 1989 she dissolved into giggles when she saw that several of the guests were resplendent in her old clothes.

When Diana first joined the family, Princess Michael, the only other really snappy Royal dresser, did try to give her some advice. But it wasn't really needed. With a little help from some of the girls on *Vogue* magazine who garnered clothes for her to try, she soon resolved her own style. She was copied by the masses from very early on and the rag trade keeps a sharp eye on what she wears. In her short time as a Princess she has launched, among other things, a million tights with butterflies embroidered on the heels and a million polka-dot pleated skirts – and that was only an inexpensive garment from a German designer Mondi which she found while browsing at Harrods. She has also given the millinery industry the best boost it has had in years.

Philip Somerville is Diana's favourite hat designer and she came across him in rather an extraordinary way. She was watching television and spotted a hat she really liked – in an advertisement for vodka. Her hairdresser discovered for her that the Cossack-style hat was made by a milliner named Philip L. Somerville.

'I was sitting in my office,' he recalls, 'and the telephone rang. It was my assistant who informed me that the Princess of Wales was in the showroom downstairs.'

Since then Philip Somerville has made most of her hats as well as the Queen's (he also has Bobo's blessing), and the Duchess of Kent's.

Diana's current favourite designer is Catherine Walker, a young French widow who lives in London. She and the Princess are uncannily alike, both tall, both shy in manner and both elegant in a long, lean way. But the designer is as dark as Diana is fair.

Catherine Walker began designing for Diana in 1986 and has helped her formulate a style. The two women have become friends. It was Catherine who designed the marvellous Mary Queen of Scott's dress for a gala benefit and whose ice-blue swathed chiffon dress helped Diana out-Hollywood all the stars at the Cannes Film Festival. She also made the witty brass-buttoned tailcoat which the Princess wore for an Ascot race meeting.

'The Princess of Wales has such elegance, grace and *joie de vivre*,' Walker says. 'She does not want to be dressed to look English or French but to be suitable for her own life.'

It was Felicity Clarke of *Vogue*, a dark-haired, lively, fun lady, who introduced the Princess to the makers of the wedding dress, the Emanuels. This young designer couple also make for both the Duchess of Kent and the Duchess of York.

'Felicity Clarke telephoned us,' David Emanuel explained, 'and said that Lord Snowdon was shooting a feature on young beauties – called the Vogue English Roses. She wanted to borrow some clothes for a tall blonde. Very carefully she didn't mention which young blonde. We had a pale pink blouse with a bow, a floppy collar and a pale pink taffeta skirt which seemed to fit the bill. We sent it round to Vogue House and apparently Diana loved the outfit. She asked who the designer was and duly booked an appointment with us.'

Diana turned up at their grey and white showrooms in London's Brook Street and as the receptionist had got the name in the appointment book wrong, no one had any idea who was arriving.

'Elizabeth [the other half of the Emanuel team] went to meet her,' David recalls, 'and as soon as I saw her I thought, Good God! It's Lady Diana. That's how it all began.'

Diana has not altered her habits of popping up at her various dressmakers' premises. Nor has she given up the pleasures of shopping, which she loves. Somehow she still manages it which must be the most terrible bore for her detectives. She buys off-the-peg mini-skirts and all kinds of wild gear from designers like Kenzo, St Laurent, and Rifat Ozbeck. But these clothes are all worn strictly in private.

All the female members of the Royal Family get their shoes from Rayne, which for many years belonged to Edward Rayne who held a Royal Warrant since 1930. He recently sold out to Rosie and David Graham and they inherited, along with the rest of the business, the individual plastic lasts for the Queen, the Queen Mother and Princess Margaret (and Mrs Thatcher). With perhaps an eye to updating their image, they wrote to the Princess of Wales asking if she would like them to make a pair of lasts of her feet. They pointed they would then be able to make any design in any fabric at any time for her.

Diana jumped at the offer. Previously she had worn mostly Charles Jourdan shoes and was delighted to be able to wear something British.

Ron Hall, a veteran of the Rayne company, has worked there

for forty-six years and is in charge of the bespoke department. The lasts cast from famous feet are kept on a shelf in what is known as Ron Hall's corner at the firm's King's Cross factory. The Queen has lasts in two styles – one rather old-fashioned and square-toed, the other more almond-toed in shape.

The Queen Mother has a last which allows for her favourite style – a platform which runs the whole of the shoe. This is combined with a 3½in. stumpy heel designed to give her extra height. Since Princess Margaret is also very petite, she has much the same kind of platform along the length of her shoes. Diana has the biggest feet of the Royal women, which is not surprising since she is taller than all of them, except Princess Michael. Diana has a special foam insert placed in her shoes between the uppers and the sole for extra comfort when she has to stand for long periods. She wears three different types of heel. A low heel, a medium height heel, and a third which is a broader, more substantial medium high heel which also makes standing for a long time less painful. She never wears stiletto heels, or even ordinarily high ones because at 5ft 10in. she is only an inch shorter than Charles. With even a small heel she hits 6ft and towers over people such as President Mitterand and his wife – which can be a touch embarrassing for everyone.

The Princess of Wales has shoes and handbags made to match her every outfit. She chooses from the Rayne collections several months before they come out. Occasionally she will substitute her own materials and have a pair of shoes especially made, but they will still be at cost price.

The Princess Royal takes after her mother in that she simply is not interested in fashion. She never was. Today she dresses well, but it took her several years to get it right – something she happily admits herself. She has her grandmother's addiction to terrible old hats and truly unbecoming clothes when working about the farm, but conforms with the obligatory hat, the coat and the brooch when on her mother's business. As a young girl she was always something of a rebel and her parents tried to tidy her up. She once kept the Queen and Prince Philip waiting in the hall at Balmoral when they were going to the Highland games. When she appeared, breathless, long hair hanging sixties style, her mother said sharply: 'Why aren't you wearing a hat?'

Anne groaned. 'Must I?'

'Yes you must,' said the Queen, 'you know you look like a sheepdog without one.'

The Queen Mother is the most dramatic dresser in the family. Even well into her eighties, she still manages to look like a fairy

Princess in the evenings. She is the embodiment of a child's picture of Royalty. Her style is furbelows, frills and feathers and she has never wavered from it. It was evolved by her favourite dress designer, Norman Hartnell, and when he died there was a general rustle of dismay.

'What are we going to do about mummy?' the Queen and Princess Margaret chorused. 'Who is going to make her clothes?'

'She's very extravagant,' sighed the Queen affectionately. 'I don't know why she needs so many clothes since they all look the same.'

Which is absolutely true. Since Hartnell's death the Queen Mother has simply continued to have his original models copied over and over again.

She has always been able to carry off the most outrageously flamboyant clothes – including the ancient and bizarre headgear she wore when up to her thighs in water, fishing for salmon. For the Queen Mother the crinoline never went out of fashion, and if her style is sometimes reminiscent of the Pearly Queen, we still adore her for it.

You may have noticed that she almost always carries a floppy matching handbag, and these are made by her dressers. She gets another yard of fabric from her dressmakers and has a handbag run up at Clarence House. Nothing is carried in these handbags, just a handkerchief.

She loves jewellery – her rubies are her favourites. And her idea of bliss is going to Covent Garden to watch the ballet, with dinner in the Royal box, and dressed up for the occasion.

She always uses a little hairpiece in front when she wears a tiara. Her hair is very thin but long, falling right down her back. She rolls it up and brings wings round the side to give a bit more support to a tiara. She is rarely seen hatless in public, nor, like her daughter does she ever visit a shop. The Queen used to go to Harrods after closing-time to do her Christmas shopping but security problems and the IRA put paid to that pleasure. The last British Queen to enjoy pottering around the shops along with the public was Queen Mary who in toque, long Edwardian dress, usually purple and with long-handled umbrella, could be found in Whiteleys of Queensway (now long gone), a department store that enjoyed her custom for many years.

Prince Charles has hardly ever been into a shop in his life. Nor does he wish to. Charles is not interested in fashion, although Princess Diana did get him out of his Lobb of St James shoes and into casual, less expensive slip-ons. This means he has to buy a lot more shoes. Lobb shoes last for ever.

But Lobb is not out of favour. They still send a selection of their styles for him to consider. When he has chosen, someone arrives to check that the Prince's feet have not changed in any way from the lasts that Lobb keep in their workrooms. He prefers what he thinks of as proper shoes – sensibly, as he has to stand on his feet a great deal in his line of work. No one has ever seen the Prince without beautifully polished shoes. This is because an orderly from the Welsh Guards has the job. He arrives daily to polish both the shoes and any bits of uniform belt and buckle that need shining.

The Prince's valet does his shopping, but mostly by telephone. A call to Turnbull and Asser will bring a collection of ties winging to Kensington Palace. The Prince chooses from these, rejecting the ones he considers to be loud. Regimental and club ties are the only ones he will consider if the colours are a bit garish. But Princess Diana is inclined to buy ties for him these days and the direct call to the shop happens less often.

A new suit requires his tailor to send a selection of fabrics to Kensington Palace and afterwards to ring for an appointment to discuss style. Another phone call is made to arrange for fittings. For many years before he was married Prince Charles patronised a tailor who always turned up in the Palace courtyard in a large Rolls Royce.

'What's he in today?' he would ask his valet when the tailor was announced. And if it was the Rolls, the reaction was always the same, 'No wonder my suits cost so much.' He eventually changed his tailor.

The Palace still houses uniforms going back to Edward VII, and these are still sometimes worn by the Royal men. One of the wardrobe rooms is set aside to hold ceremonial clothing. In this room is the tailor's dummy that was originally made for George V. Charles and his great-grandfather are much of a size except that Charles' legs are longer. But his jackets fit it perfectly. The dummy is now used by artists when they are painting robes and also to check out a uniform before Prince Charles or his father wears it. Uniforms can hang for months without ever being touched. Before wearing, therefore, the valet dresses the dummy to make sure there are no buttons missing, no loose braid or any small tears on the uniform. Anything wrong, and the linen room at the Palace are called in for running repairs.

Royal men have an enormous amount of ceremonial clothing. Prince Charles, for example, is Colonel of twelve different regiments – all of which have at least four uniforms, mess dress, khaki, number ones (worn on ceremonial occasions) and tropical whites.

In fact, there are eight outfits alone for his rank of Commander in the Royal Navy, once you add in tropical whites and other variations. There are also Naval and Air Force uniforms in the same ratio and Scottish regimental kilts, quite apart from all the various robes for the Order of the Garter, Order of the Thistle and Order of the Bath. There are also parliamentary robes and robes connected with honorary university degrees. All of these are worn with different decorations, and it is a formidable task for a valet to learn which bits go where. It is essential he gets it right though, since if all the medals and so forth are not in the right place the regiment (or organisation) concerned will be offended.

A new set of robes costs the earth, therefore all these rarely worn garments are carefully looked after. Just a scarlet guards' tunic costs well over a £1,000, so when a new uniform or set of robes are made they are made to last a century. Sometimes the robes last even longer. A retired valet or a retired footman comes in regularly to check the robes over. A working valet has quite enough to do without all that.

The late Lord Mountbatten adored uniforms and dressing up in them. And it was he, Charles' 'honorary grandfather', who instilled in the Prince a respect for uniforms and their ceremonial significance. Mountbatten's creed was 'if you've got it, wear it'. This meant that on ceremonial occasions the much decorated Earl went on parade looking, as he gleefully put it, 'like a Christmas tree'. At Lord Mountbatten's funeral, the bereaved Prince Charles grimly pinned on every decoration that he was entitled to on to his uniform.

'Lord Mountbatten would have liked it,' he said. 'And if the IRA want to get me through the heart, they'll have a job.'

All that clothing also gives an idea of the Prince of Wales' many responsibilities. It's not surprising that one morning, not long before he married, he borrowed the key to the wardrobe room, which is just along the corridor from the rooms he once occupied in the Palace.

'I just want to show Lady Diana the number of uniforms I have,' he told his valet. It was a subtle way of showing her exactly how much his job entails.

Today all those one hundred or so uniforms have been moved to Kensington Palace where there is a uniform room.

Prince Charles is not the least bit interested in jewellery. He does own five exceedingly good watches and several pairs of fine cufflinks, but these were handed down from his great-grandfather

142

via his grandfather. The finest thing he owns is the diamond Garter insignia which he wears only on State occasions. This, too, belonged to his grandfather, George V, and was originally a present from Queen Victoria. These days Royalty give each other simple presents. The Victorians did not. Gifts of expensive jewellery were the norm when Victoria was on the throne – which is one of the reasons why the family own so much today.

Before Charles married, Bobo who has charge of the Queen's amazing collection of jewellery said to him, almost finger to lip, 'I'll have a look through the Queen's jewellery for you. She's got so many pieces she never uses. We'll pick something out for Lady Diana.'

Before her engagement Diana had only a gold chain with a 'D' hanging from it and a couple of pairs of ear-rings.

One morning when the opportunity presented itself, Bobo rang down to Prince Charles and said: 'Come up and see me as soon as you can. I've got the jewellery out.'

The old Scottish maid and the future King spent a couple of hours poring over the folding layers of trays full of quite remarkable jewellery. Charles picked out the pieces that he thought his future bride would most like and later Bobo, with the pieces all carefully put together, said to the Queen: 'Why don't we give these to Charles to give to Diana?'

It didn't work out quite like that. They were given to Diana, but the Queen presented them herself, bit by bit. She saw Diana for lunch frequently before the wedding, and each time her future daughter-in-law came away from the Palace with a not inconsiderable trinket.

Not unnaturally, Diana was delighted.

She also loves costume jewellery and now owns a veritable treasure chest of baubles, bangles and beads which she mixes with the real thing with great panache.

Another member of the Royal Family with great style is Princess Michael of Kent. When she broke her wrist in a ski-ing accident early in 1989, the plaster-of-Paris cast was unsightly to her well-trained eye. She got her dressmaker to run up a series of little 'coats' to cover the cast. These were made in all different colours and fabrics to match whatever she was wearing.

Princess Michael not only has a good eye but she is perfectly capable of making her own clothes – to couture standard. As a young girl in Australia with very little money, she was always the best dressed of her friends because she could copy anything from fashion magazines. She can even cut her own patterns.

Today most of her clothes come from Gianfranco Ferre who specialises in outfits for the tall silhouette. Her sister-in-law, the Duchess of Kent, like Princess Diana prefers to stick to English designers. Strangely enough it was the Duchess who discovered the Emanuels, Victor Edelstein, the couturier, and Catherine Walker long before the Princess of Wales ever thought of using them.

Those who dress and groom the Royals are a small, loyal group. And the hairdressers who also share intimate relationships with their clients.

Hugh of Ebury Street tends Princess Michael's streaked blonde hair (she is really a brunette) and the Duchess of Kent who also lightens her hair. They are not alone. Diana streaks her mousy hair and the Queen uses a tint called 'chocolate kiss' to cover the grey. She also emphasises some of the grey at her temples, taking the advice of Charles Martyn, her hairdresser of many years.

Michael of Michaeljohn has dealt with Princess Anne's hair for years and used to have Fergie as a client. But his stylist, Denise McAdam, became so close to the Duchess that she was able to leave and start her own business in nearby Hay Hill and the Duchess went with her. Richard Dalton, Princess Diana's hairdresser who started at Headlines, got the job permanently when Kevin Shanley, Diana's original hairdresser, made the mistake of talking too freely to the press. Dalton still tends Diana's hair and has recently opened a salon of his own in Claridges Hotel.

For all the hairdressers, valets and dressers the best perk of all is travelling with their illustrious Royal employers. They get to go on the Royal Yacht, the Royal train and in aircraft of the Queen's Flight. They are at Balmoral, Windsor and Sandringham for the shooting. They travel abroad on State visits and meet some of the most powerful and glamorous people in the world.

As Richard Dalton once said, 'Once my secret ambition was to style Elizabeth Taylor's hair. I never imagined I would end up as hairdresser to the future Queen of England.'

# Escape

The Royal Family are deprived of many aspects of normal life but time off for play is not one of them. Quite unashamedly when it comes to holidays the Monarch and her relatives behave more like the idle aristocracy than a working Royal Family.

They take six weeks off from before Christmas and into the New Year, and over Easter enjoy nearly a fortnight at Windsor. Ascot Week, when the Court goes to Windsor, is in June and cannot really be considered hard work. The following month, the Royal Yacht Britannia takes them on their annual Scottish Western Isles cruise to begin their main ten week summer holiday which is always spent in Scotland.

The Royal weekend is not bad, either. It starts after lunch on Friday afternoons and ends mid-morning Monday.

For the men of the family, there always seems to be plenty of time in the week for hunting, carriage driving, polo and other assorted pleasures.

Prince Charles often manages to hunt four times a week. When he is at Highgrove he goes out with the Beaufort, the Berkeley or the Bicester packs, all of which are within reasonable distance of his Gloucestershire home. He spends Wednesdays and Saturdays with the Belvoir in Lincolnshire, and Mondays and Fridays with the Quorn. He is not alone in taking this kind of time off. At times his father manages at least a couple of days a week practising his carriage driving when he is not abroad.

When we are told that a member of the family has undertaken

145

a large number of engagements, no one mentions that some of those engagements will have taken the particular Royal a short, sharp ten minutes, in their own quarters, chatting with someone who has called simply to be presented or who might be about to contribute to one of their pet charities.

No one would deny that being Royal, when on duty, is pressure-filled and obviously the Royal Family are entitled to holidays. But do these have to be quite so sacrosanct?

Not one member of the Royal Family attended the memorial service for those who died in the Lockerbie disaster – when an American jumbo jet was blown out of the sky by a terrorist bomb and ripped the heart out of the small Scottish border town. Many people were outraged and hurt by the insensitive behaviour of the Royals, but what could they expect when the service took place at a time when the Royal Family were cosily tucked up at Sandringham, enjoying their annual six weeks of pheasant shooting?

It took weeks to even begin to repair the damage they had inflicted on their own prestige. The Queen did make a private donation to the disaster appeal fund but the unthinking Royals had made a terrible mistake. And it was not helped either by Prince Philip's presence at Emperor Hirohito's funeral in Japan so soon afterwards.

Eventually, Prince Charles went up to Scotland on the Royal train and, as ever, did his best to dispel the resentment in the stricken town. He did so with great skill, great dignity and considerable success. But an 'about time, too' feeling lingered on.

Not only are Royal holidays long, they are spectacular. There is Britannia to play with, which is like owning a luxurious ocean liner and not having to pay for the crew. The Royal Yacht does lack a swimming pool and a ballroom but not many cruise liners have the same ratio of staff and sailors to guests as Britannia. Every July the Queen sets sail for the ten-day traditional Western Isles cruise with a full complement of an admiral, 277 sailors, close members of her family (each with their own personal staff), and the band of the Royal Marines.

Also on board is the Lord High Admiral, but this happens to be the Queen herself.

The Queen joins the yacht at Southampton on the last Friday evening in July. She travels by rail from Waterloo in a Royal carriage attached to an ordinary InterCity express. While she is on the train the yacht makes its stately way up Southampton Water from the Isle of Wight where Prince Philip and a party of family and friends have already spent the last three or four days enjoying Cowes Week – another small holiday.

The Queen has little interest in sailing and stays at Windsor while Prince Philip, using the Royal Yacht as his base, is messing about in boats. He is a Commodore and very much involved at Cowes. Her Majesty might undertake a few official engagements, but basically this week tends to be a winding-down time before beginning the holiday proper.

In London, Buckingham Palace starts closing up. Staff prepare the vast building for its summer face-lift, emptying rooms ready for their redecoration. Repair work on Royal homes is usually carried out while the Queen is taking her Scottish holiday.

The Western Isles cruise begins with the Band of the Royal Marines playing at Southampton Docks as the Queen is piped aboard Britannia. The crew await her lined up in their best blues. As the Admiral steps forward to welcome her, telescope firmly under his arm, Prince Philip's standard flutters down and the Queen's is raised in its place. The Lord High Admiral is aboard and the lady is in charge.

As Prince Charles once joked – How many people can claim two admirals as parents? In addition to his mother being the Lord High Admiral, his father is an Admiral of the Fleet. Charles and brother Andrew are both Navy men, so when the Royal Yacht sets off on her voyage around Britain she has three extra experienced sailors aboard.

For the trip the Queen takes her own cooks, Pages and footmen who arrive with all their livery. They take over from the Britannia crew who have been looking after Prince Philip's party during the previous week. Throughout the day, her staff have been bringing the luggage on board while her chefs were taking over the yacht's galley from the naval cooks. Though the naval crew is highly efficient, the Queen likes to have her own staff to look after her.

Britannia is the Queen's floating Palace and she takes aboard everything that might possibly be needed. Nothing is left on the ship between trips except possibly some old clothes. The Royal quarters are simple, but comfortable. The furniture is upholstered in greys and beiges. The carpets are grey and the paintwork white. The Queen and Prince Philip occupy the two main bedrooms and a dressing-room. Princess Diana borrowed this dressing-room to use during her honeymoon voyage.

The corridors on the Royal deck are lined with drawings of previous Royal Yachts and a collection of family photographs that have been taken on board. All of them are the work of the yacht's official photographer. He is on board to record all the happy scenes, and family photographs are taken every year. These are framed and added to the others along the corridors to show how the children have grown over the years. The collection goes back to when Charles and Anne were little.

What the Royal Family constantly seek is privacy and quiet, and on this trip – if the weather stays calm – that is what they find. On board all is tranquil and even the sailors wear gym shoes as part of their special effort to keep the peace. Only the closest members of the family are invited – the Queen's children and grandchildren, Princess Margaret with her children, Princess Alexandra, who is the Royals' favourite Royal, and just occasionally some of the Duke's German relations.

It is all very well to find privacy at sea but with it comes unpredictable weather. Britannia usually keeps ploughing along. Though the Admiral might occasionally stop somewhere remote, perhaps in Wales or on the Isle of Man, the Royals seldom go ashore until they get to the Western Isles. Just occasionally the Queen might carry out an official or semi-official duty, but mostly they just keep on sailing.

Although the Yacht rarely puts into port on this trip, there are always fresh flowers aboard. They are taken on at Southampton and kept in a cold room. There is also enough food in the larder for the ship's cooks to produce, if need be, a banquet.

When Britannia leaves Southampton she heads west along the south coast of England past Bournemouth and on, round Land's End, up through St George's Channel steadily steaming north until the Western Isles are near. Then the pattern is to sail at night and anchor during the day in a loch or the shadow of an island. The family have their regular favourite stopping places and rain or shine eat a picnic lunch ashore every day. Only when the sea is too rough for the Royal barge to reach the coast in comfort do they lunch on board.

They do try to pick landing places with a jetty so that the party can land without having to wade through water.

The Royal barge is lowered halfway down the ship's side on cables. Then a gangway is put across for boarding so that dignity is always maintained. There is a lift from the Royal quarters to take them down to the mid-level where the barge waits.

Ashore they settle for simple food such as egg starters, cold meats and salads. Drinks go ashore in containers. As well as spirits there will be burgundy and Moselle, their favourite white wine. The only person who might spot them sitting on their heavy car rugs in the heather is the occasional crofter, but he's probably seen them every year anyway, and is not inclined to take much notice.

The Admiral is sometimes invited but if he has not been on the picnic he waits to welcome the Queen back aboard, again with his telescope under his arm. Her Majesty then takes tea on the verandah deck, under glass, where she has a fine view of the escort vessel and it has a fine view of her. But like the crofter, those aboard the guardian escort dutifully turn a blind eye.

Younger members of the family spend most of their time afloat in this glass sitting-room on the deck above the formal drawing room. They like to eat out here so they can watch the view slide by.

It is on this holiday where she is so relaxed that the Queen can be seen wearing navy blue trousers. Never jeans. She leaves those to Princess Anne and Princess Diana who wears the fun, patterned sweaters that she collects, topped with an anorak and tailed with canvas sailing shoes from Captain Watt in Dover Street.

Although lunch ashore is eaten in macs and waterproofs, dinner each night is a dignified occasion. The Queen wears a long dress, though possibly rather an old one which has been seen before in public. Prince Charles and Prince Philip will wear black tie and their Royal Thames Squadron mess jackets. They eat in the formal dining room with a string orchestra playing throughout the meal. Below decks, the jazz section of the Royal Marine band plays for the crew.

Normally the Queen eats by candlelight but for safety reasons there are no candles on the yacht and the magnificent silver candelabrum have electric bulbs, wired from under the table.

In a bad storm the ship can be very uncomfortable. Noisy, too, with a lot of crashing and banging. Prince Philip is by far the best sailor of the family. When the ship starts to roll, the ladies retire to their cabins, and so do most of the men. But not Prince Philip. He rides through it and if it is time to eat, he eats, with the staff desperately sliding and rolling with the ship's movement as they endeavour to serve him his meal.

Dinner creates an opportunity for the Queen to meet her ship's officers and two or three are invited every night – a flag officer who usually goes on to greater things, and, of course, the Admiral. The Captain of the accompanying destroyer or frigate is always invited to pop over at least once.

After dinner the Queen leads the way from the ship's dining room and through to the drawing room for coffee. This room has a fireplace, but only for show. While the officers are making polite conversation with their Lord High Admiral, staff will be breaking down the dining table and stowing the pieces in niches under the windows. Then the dining chairs are lined up and a film is shown – usually a new one, sent to the Queen with the compliments of the film company.

One evening, during the journey, the Queen and her family will go to the wardroom and dine with the officers. This is the highspot of the cruise for the officers' mess. The Royal chef is out of a job that night; the Navy cook takes over, and there is quite a bit of gentle rivalry.

Downstairs the Queen's staff will be socialising, too, asking the petty officers to drinks while other messes are having their own parties and entertaining different groups of those on board.

There are strict demarcation lines. The Queen never goes below the level of the top deck. The fore of the ship is her territory, the stern belongs to the crew, and never the twain meet. But Princess Diana roamed the whole ship when she was on her honeymoon, and Prince Charles left her to it. He, too, knows the ship inside out from his childhood days.

The Royal children always join the Queen's summer cruise, and like any inquisitive youngster they explore everywhere from the engine room to the bridge. As a boy, Andrew regarded this as a great treat and was the ring-leader of his own gang of small Royals. William is now taking over this role.

There is a proper little shop on the second deck, run by the NAAFI where everything is sold at NAAFI prices. William and Harry are allowed to buy sweets with their pocket money from this shop, though it really exists for crew to buy postcards and souvenirs of the yacht. When he was small, Andrew loved to get down to the stores in the bowels of the ship where he and his brother, Edward, were given gym shoes, jeans and blue naval pullovers. They would run around in this miniature uniform with great pride.

On the Queen's instructions, all the children have to wear a life-jacket on board. They are each also allocated a sailor whose thankless job it is not only to keep them out of mischief but prevent the unthinkable – falling overboard. The sailor looks after the same child for the entire trip and has to answer endless questions. Some of the young ones, like the energetic Prince Andrew in his day or Prince William now, are more of a responsibility than others.

Aboard Britannia, there is plenty to do. A motor boat waits to be let down over the side if anyone wants a ride. Prince Charles windsurfs, and Fergie and Andrew water ski or play water polo. None of them is into deep-sea fishing, though the children appear aft to watch the crew fish. Because there is no proper swimming pool the children make do with a giant inflated rubber tyre. They have great fun in this enormous paddling pool which is six feet deep and has room to swim about a bit. It is kept on the top deck where there is also a chance to play deck hockey or deck quoits.

A particularly exciting time for the children is when the weather is too bad for a helicopter to drop in with the Queen's mail and the escort vessel comes alongside to deliver it. In rough weather the post is passed backwards and forwards from ship to ship via a rope with a sliding sling. This is strong enough to hold a sailor, and it is the children's idea of heaven to be allowed to take the hairy ride. It is not permitted until they are twelve years old, so Prince William and Harry still have a long wait.

It is never warm enough to swim from Britannia on this cruise because the sea is always so cold but when it is warm enough on other occasions there is a special ladder for the use of swimmers.

Princess Diana who had the run of the Royal Yacht for her honeymoon made good use of these steps, swimming every day in the Mediterranean. Wearing a bikini, she would swim alone at one end of the yacht while the sailors swam a respectful distance away. Prince Charles stayed on deck sunbathing, determined to get a tan. Someone had told him that suntan lotions are bad for the skin so he refused to use one, insisting that his skin could take it. It was interesting that he did not get burned but he certainly did get tanned.

The honeymooners spent most of the time on the open verandah which is off the glassed-in sunroom. The Princess cultivated her tan, and she and her new husband sat there to cool off in the evenings.

It was a magic time for the couple. One night in Greece the wardroom gave a barbecue for the newly-weds on a moonlit beach while Britannia gently rode at anchor in the bay. The chef, Mervyn, was given the night off to attend the festivities and the naval officers did all the cooking. Everyone swam and after the meal a barge arrived bearing the accordionist from the Royal Marine band. The officers handed out song sheets and the whole party enjoyed a sing-song around a fire built from driftwood on the sand.

The Princess has a good singing voice, and she and her dresser Evelyn, the only other woman aboard, sang the soprano parts, their voices bell-like in the quiet stillness of the night.

Sometimes Prince Charles and his bride went ashore. The Admiral would consult with them daily as to where he thought they might like to swim and picnic, suggesting places that were private, deserted and with a good beach.

Since it was all something of a holiday for many of the staff and crew as well, there were parties going on all over the ship. The Prince's chef, his detectives and his valet decided that they would give their own Pimms party for the crew and were in the kitchen cutting up the fruit when Princess Diana's head came around the door, wanting to know what they were up to.

Hearing there was to be a party she said, 'That sounds like fun. Can I come?'

It was agreed that she could come, but the valet tactfully said perhaps it would be a good idea if she didn't mention it to the Prince. His presence would have changed the evening into a formal one with everyone having to be on their best behaviour.

'Oh, that's all right,' Diana said – and came on her own.

A mixed bag of guests had been invited – from the Admiral down to representatives from the stokers' mess. The stokers were surprised to see the Admiral, and the Admiral was amazed to see them. For a moment, the hosts were afraid that someone might get stuffy, but the Princess saved the day. She grabbed a jug of Pimms and took it over to the stokers and put them at their ease. Indeed, she herself seemed to be having more fun with the young ratings who were nearer her own age than the ship's officers.

On another occasion she had been ordering the day's meals from the chef when she spotted the two policemen and the valet heading for the crew's quarters. She seemed to be looking for something to do and said, 'Can I come with you?'

When she came into the mess, a great cheer went up from the sailors and every man jack of them stood to attention. A bit startled by the din, she hesitated, then grinned and dived into the crowd.

'Please sit down,' she called out, and when they did a piano was revealed.

'Who plays?' she asked. No one volunteered, but some brave soul shouted: 'Give us a tune then.'

She plonked herself down on the piano stool and played Greensleeves while thirty sailors bellowed out the words. The new Princess of Wales was thoroughly enjoying herself, but the officers got wind that she was there, and came and gently led her away.

A highlight of any Royal cruise is always the ship's concert. A stage is created on the foc'sle and it is Royal Concert Party night with everyone aboard invited. The Royal Family have armchairs in the front row, with their Household on hard chairs behind them.

Even the crew who are on duty sit at the back. The cast of sailors write the material themselves, spend a lot of time rehearsing, and they dress up, mostly in jokey drag. The acts consist of a light sending up of everything, including some in the Royal Family – but never ever the Queen. Prince Charles has appeared himself in the ship's concert. He once did a goon act and ended up blowing bubbles from a bubble pipe – an act he had perfected while at Cambridge University.

On the honeymoon, one large sailor was dressed up as Princess Diana in the famous see-through frock of her kindergarten days and making rather rude jokes. The Princess, laughing in her armchair, loved every minute of it.

A lot of the entertainment aboard comes from the ship's radio. The wireless room picks up ordinary stations and there is also a ship's own channel, run by the radio officers. They compile a ship's quiz and all sections are supposed to take part – the Royals, the staff, and all the eight different messes.

There are twenty-five questions to answer and it has been known for the stokers to win, beating the Royals.

News comes via the wireless room, too. Each morning there is a newsheet rather like a telex message on the breakfast table. There is no television, but there is video, and a piano – mainly for Princess Margaret's use.

Even at sea Royal business still goes on. As well as delivering the post, RAF helicopters drop the newspapers on board every couple of days. They hover in front of the bridge, dropping boxes and letters and picking up any urgent mail for delivery.

A little booklet is issued on life afloat and left in everyone's cabin. There are no lifeboat drills; everyone is expected to know where their lifeboat is. The Queen can hardly fail to know where her barge is. Instructions on what to do in an emergency are part of the contents of the booklet.

For the Royals, a highspot of the cruise is the visit to have lunch and tea with the Queen Mother at the Castle of Mey. The Queen Mother herself comes to meet them at the jetty, invariably wearing a kilt in either Balmoral or Royal Stuart tartan. The entire family then start wearing their kilts. The Royal rule is that no one should wear a kilt south of Perth.

A fleet of cars brings everyone back to the castle and very often some of the staff are asked to lunch, too, though they eat separately. The Queen Mother realises that it is a treat for the people on board to get ashore. Lunch is fairly late and then the guests look at the beautiful garden or perhaps take a walk on the beach which lies below the castle before coming back for tea.

The Queen Mother again goes to see everyone off and is back home in time to wave goodbye to the yacht as it steams past at about 7.30p.m. sailing as close in as possible to shore. There is always a house-party at the castle, and the guests will come out on to the path that runs down to the beach to watch the yacht sail away.

As Britannia passes, she sends up flares, and the display is reciprocated with more flares from the castle which also has people waving huge linen bed sheets out of the windows. Sometimes though, the weather is far too misty to see much except the fireworks.

On from then on it is straight sailing to Aberdeen where around 14 August the Royals generally arrive to a smell of kippers and to be met by the Queen's corgis. The Royal Yacht is the one place in Britain where they are never taken. And at the dock, a fleet of cars is waiting to take everyone off to Balmoral.

The staff who were left behind in London will have been busy packing and sending the luggage to Balmoral with considerable help from the Army.

The cruise is over and the second part of the summer holidays begins as the yacht starts sailing back down the east coast to home base at Portsmouth.

The sailors draw lots for places on one of the old Andovers of the Queen's Flight which flies home the staff who are not going on to Balmoral. Any spare seats go to the crew – not the officers. This is considered a great perk because if their number comes up they get home four days early. The Queen and Charles settle down with a sigh at their favourite place in the world.

The ten-week Royal holiday in Scotland is basically one long house-party, but for the younger members of the family Balmoral has not quite the razzmatazz of smart Verbier in Switzerland where Fergie once presided over her own dining table or the sunshine of King Carlos' summer home on Mallorca where Princess Diana escapes with the children each summer. Fergie, who had been hostess at quite a few house-parties herself in her day, adjusted more rapidly to the routine of this Scottish holiday than did Diana. Balmoral is formal, stuffy and yet in some ways quite ordinary. None of the Queen's private homes are grand. At Balmoral the stone-floor entrance hall is dominated by a bust of Queen Victoria who stares at the litter of fishing rods, waterproof clothing, wellington boots and dog bowls. The Queen personally feeds her dogs there. Step on into the red-carpeted inner hall and there is an equally disapproving and enormous statue of Victoria's husband, Prince Albert.

Dull it may be, but Balmoral is a haven to the Royal Family. It sits in the middle of nowhere, by the River Dee, in one of the most beautiful parts of Scotland. Once behind the Castle's Scottish Baronial walls, and surrounded by its 50,000 acres, the Royal Family are safe from prying eyes. The press cannot get at them and they can settle down to living in their own somewhat archaic style.

It is here that the Queen indulges in one of her hobbies – star-gazing. In the clear, high northern sky at night, she often points out and names the stars of the heavens to her guests. She has a genuine interest in, and knowledge of, astronomy.

An astronomer royal, indeed.

The Balmoral holiday has been used as examination time for both prospective Royal wives and Royal husbands. Some of Prince Charles' girlfriends did not pass the test of relentless open-air activities, regardless of the weather. Diana passed in the courting days but once she was Princess of Wales it became obvious that Balmoral and all the shooting and fishing and picnicking in a freezing wind bored her rigid. She seemed, too, to suffer withdrawal symptoms if she were too far away from Harrods, and she took to fleeing back to London.

But as time has passed she has come to appreciate that this magnificent part of Scotland is one of the few places where it is almost – only almost – possible for the Royal Family to enjoy a private life.

Also, the arrival of the Duchess of York on the Royal stage helped ease the tedium of endless, wet Balmoral holidays and last year, with her friend Fergie for companionship, Diana was content to spend time with baby Beatrice and take the young Princes swimming in the hotel's pool nearby.

She did attempt to join in with the pursuits of shooting and stalking, but although she was 'blooded' by the Balmoral Ghillie and proved herself a reasonable shot, public criticism and anti-bloodsport leagues cut short her enjoyment of these most Royal of pastimes. Fergie goes out with Andrew and, always keen to develop a new skill, has had a few shooting lessons. Taking a tip from Diana, though, she has not pursued these any further.

Not a great deal happens at Balmoral, or indeed at Sandringham where the Royals spend the winter holiday.

The highlight of the Scottish break is the Ghillies' Ball. There

155

are two, actually, one given by the Queen and the other by the Queen Mother. These summer dances are given for the Scottish staff and neighbours. The Queen's takes place in the Ballroom at Balmoral at ten in the evening, after dinner. All the Royal Family dress up to the nines. The men are in the kilt and the women wear tiaras and Stuart tartan sashes over their white evening dresses. Everyone is there from the beaters to the local aristocracy.

The Queen's house-party guests attend and do their duty by dancing with the estate workers. There is no apartheid here. A favourite number is the Paul Jones where the Royals move around in the circle with everyone else and when the music stops change partners to dance with whoever fate throws their way. During a Paul Jones, Queen Fabiola of the Belgians found herself facing and then dancing off with the estate carpenter.

Politely, she asked what he did.

'I'm the estate carpenter, Your Highness,' he told her.

Queen Fabiola looked puzzled. 'Carpenter? Carpenter?' she said frowning, and then her expression brightened. 'Ah, carpenter!' she said triumphant. 'My husband would have liked to be a carpenter if he wasn't the King.'

Which left the carpenter somewhat puzzled. 'Imagine,' he said the next day. 'He'd rather have been a carpenter!'

There is little formality at these balls. The Queen Mother once asked a soldier guest to dance with her. Embarrassed, he explained that he was booked for the Queen. The Queen Mother cheerfully danced off with someone else and as she passed her daughter and her partner, tapped him on the shoulder and said: 'Snob!'

The elders of the Royal party always leave after the midnight interval when supper is served. They know that once they have gone people will have a better time since they no longer have to be on their best behaviour. All the Royal Family are aware of this, and never stay to the end at any gathering, unless it is a close family one. But everyone else, including the younger members of the Royal Family, dances on until two in the morning and with no shortage of alcohol everyone lets their hair down.

The Queen Mother's ball is a most generous one and after midnight the alcohol really flows. Nothing changes with this particular evening. Each year it is the same band, the Jack Sinclair band from Glasgow, the same tunes, the same dances and certainly the same hostess. When she leaves after the midnight interval, without fail she goes up to the bandleader and says, 'Thank you so much, Mr

Sinclair, you won't mind playing on to the end, will you?' And without fail he says, 'Oh no, Ma'am.'

The Queen Mother does not like change.

And something else that does not change is that after her Ghillies' Ball the roads to Balmoral are littered with cars that have been sensibly abandoned, their owners having decided that it would be more advisable to walk.

Because there is not a great deal for someone like Diana to do at Balmoral, for the last three years she has insisted on a pre-Balmoral break at the summer palace of King Juan Carlos of Spain. For a week or ten days Diana, Charles, William and Harry fly to Mallorca for a bucket-and-spade holiday. Diana loves it and so do the children. Their days are spent on the beach, by the pool or on Juan Carlos' powerful yacht. Charles, who likes the sunshine, also enjoys himself and once the heat of the day has subsided takes himself off into the olive groves with a sketch pad and captures the local scenery when the light is at its best.

Charles often leaves Diana and the children to spend a few extra days in Mallorca while he flies home to do some fishing in Iceland with Lady Tryon and her husband or, more likely, on the River Dee in the company of his grandmother, the Queen Mother.

It is interesting that while Princess Diana cannot bear to be away from London for too long, Prince Charles is the same about Scotland and the gentle hills that surround Balmoral.

# The Head That
# Wears The Crown

Royalty – and most particularly the Queen – know that if the Monarchy is to survive they must insist upon the bended knee from the lower orders and often from those closest to them. Respect for the Monarchy as an institution is what keeps them going in a changing world. In public, even her own mother, sister and daughter must curtsey to the Queen.

It was an accident of history which put the Queen on the throne, yet today no one could be more regal. Her dedication to the Monarchy has always set her apart.

This she learned when her father reluctantly became King George VI after the abdication of Edward VIII. The, then, new Queen Elizabeth, now the Queen Mother, insisted that her two small daughters, Princess Elizabeth and Princess Margaret Rose, curtsey to their father.

The King, a simple man, protested that this was not necessary. But his wife was adamant. The children must understand, she said, that the Monarchy is above all things – even family and private life.

Our future Queen learned the lesson well and still obeys its teachings today. Never for one instant does she forget that she is the Monarch, not just of the United Kingdom, but of ten nations. Her grand full rank and title is:

Elizabeth the Second, by the Grace of God, of the United Kingdom of Great Britain, Northern Ireland and her Other Realms and Territories, Queen, Head of the Commonwealth and Defender of the Faith.

She was the first Sovereign to be proclaimed Head of the Commonwealth. She has more than a billion subjects.

Is it not surprising that she can get a bit grand at times?

John Barratt, who was secretary to Lord Mountbatten for many years, recalls an early meeting with the Queen and Prince Philip. They were visiting the Mountbatten's Hampshire home, Broadlands, for the weekend. John Barratt strode into the drawing room with the day's letters to be signed, not realising the Queen and her husband were sitting there.

'Oh, is that this evening's work?' Mountbatten said, and turning to the Queen added, 'You remember my secretary, Barratt?'

Barratt bowed, but made the mistake of murmuring, 'Good evening, Your Royal Highness.'

Prince Philip roared with laughter. 'You've demoted Her Majesty!' he said.

Embarrassed, John remembered that the Queen (and her mother) must be called Your Majesty. The lowlier Royals are HRH. His apology was graciously accepted. But he never made the same mistake again.

The Queen expects to be properly addressed because she has always lived by the rules her mother taught her. From an early age she understood the mystery of the Monarchy and appreciated that it must be protected.

Since she was crowned Queen on 2 June 1953 she has lived a life where only a handful of people can call her by a familiar name. Her husband calls her darling. Her four children call her mummy. Her five grandchildren call her granny. Her own mother, her sister and a sprinkling of foreign royalty, plus her personal maid, Bobo Macdonald, call her by her childhood name, Lilibet.

Princess Margaret's children call her Auntie Lilibet. The rest of the family, like the rest of the world must address her as Your Majesty or Ma'am.

Perhaps something that best describes the limitations of her life is to know that even at a Royal party, where, like any family in the land, all her family wear paper crowns and funny hats, the Queen still wears a real tiara. Not for an instant can she let dignity desert her.

She, and the rest of her relatives who are entitled to call themselves HRH must remain largely distant and aloof from the real world. Familiarity would indeed risk contempt. Bicycling for photographers, as the Dutch Royal Family do, is not for British Royalty.

The Monarchy still has teeth. It is not all pomp and circumstance.

The Queen has many powers. She can dissolve Parliament if the need should arise. The Law and defence of the Realm belong to her. It is Her Majesty's Government, the Queen's Bench, and Her Majesty's Armed Forces. The Post Office is hers, and the Coast Guard. She is even the Lord High Admiral. She has the right to declare war, and she could lay about her creating Lords if she so desired. Mercifully, she is unlikely to do either. Much more important from her point of view is that the ordinary people trust her and write to her with their problems as if she were some regal agony aunt.

And she really does read the letters she receives. Letters from strangers are known as 'dead letters' in the Palace and the Queen reads them while sitting under the hairdryer in her curlers. They are brought to her in an old-fashioned straw basket which sits at the side of her chair while she flips through every letter. Each one is acknowledged. The Queen's Ladies-in-Waiting reply to those from children. More serious letters are dealt with by her private secretary and truly serious ones go to the Home Office. A letter to the Queen can get results. They are passed on with a note that Her Majesty would like to know the progress of this matter and it is amazing how swiftly the Government Department concerned moves into action.

Over the years of her reign, other members of the family have taken their turn in wearing the crown of public popularity, or sometimes had to face public disfavour. But the Queen's popularity does not waver.

She never forgets that among her many other styles and titles she is defender of the faith. And for this and many other reasons, reaching the age when most women retire will make little difference to her. When Elizabeth II, by the grace of God, came to the throne, she was crowned and annointed Queen in a solemn, religious ceremony. Not only did she make her vows to her people. She made them to God. It is possible that deep in her heart she would like nothing better than to hand the Crown and its responsibilities to Prince Charles and go quietly into retirement. But it is unlikely that she will ever abdicate even though Prince Charles shares her dedication to 'the job'. He will make a fine King when the time comes. But those who know him say he is in no hurry for this to happen. He realises the restrictions of the Crown will severely curb his opportunities to influence the future of his country. He is also surprisingly lacking in ambition for power. After some false starts he has found a positive role for himself in what amounts to the preservation of the nation and all that is good in British life.

160

The time when his views were regarded as cranky has passed. He was ahead of his time. The Press and public now listen to what he has to say. He knows that once he is King it will no longer be possible to be so forthright.

But there is no doubt that all his life he will put the Nation first. Just as the Queen has done. In 1947, when she came of age, she said: 'I declare before you all that my whole life, whether it be long or short, shall be devoted to your service.'

She has always kept that promise.

Never once has she faltered. Little wonder that in this cynical world the roar can still be heard: God Save The Queen.

# Bibliography

Barry, Stephen, *Royal Secrets* (Villard Books, 1985)
Barry, Stephen, *Royal Service* (Macmillan, 1983)
Courtney, Nicholas, *Royal Children* (Dent, 1982)
Courtney, Nicholas, *The Sporting Royals* (Hutchinson, 1983)
Hall, Unity, *Philip the Man Behind the Monarchy* (Michael O'Mara Books, 1987)
Hamilton, Alan, *The Royal Handbook* (Mitchell Beazley, 1985)
Hamilton, Alan, *The Real Charles* (Collins, 1988)
Hoey, Brian, *Princess Anne* (Country Life, 1984)
Hoey, Brian, *Monarchy* (BBC, 1987)
Junor, Penny, *Charles* (Sidgwick and Jackson, 1987)
Lacey, Robert, *Majesty* (Hutchinson, 1977)
Menkes, Suzy, *The Royal Jewels* (Grafton, 1985)
Morton, Andrew, *Inside Kensington Palace* (Michael O'Mara Books, 1987)
Morton, Andrew, *Duchess* (Michael O'Mara Books, 1988)
Oliver, Charles, *Dinner at Buckingham Palace* (Prentice-Hall, Inc, 1972)
Parker, Eileen, *Step Aside for Royalty* (Bachman & Turner, 1982)
Seward, Ingrid, *Diana* (Weidenfeld & Nicolson, 1988)

# Index

Adeane, Edward, 129
Aga Khan, 98
Alexandra, Princess, 40, 90–91, 98;
    husband and children of, 6, 28,
    56, 57; and royal family, 2, 10,
    148
'Allah' (nanny), 25
Althorp, 17–18
Amin, Idi, 130
Amner Hall, 2
Annabel's (nightclub), 81, 116
Anderson, John, 63
Anderson, Mabel, 25, 30, 31, 35, 56,
    64–65
Andrew, Prince *see* York, Duke of
Anne, Princess *see* Princess Royal
Antigua, 98
Armstrong-Jones, Lady Sarah, 17,
    28, 57, 78
Ascot, Royal, 65, 145

Baden, Margrave of, 17
Badminton House, 96
Ballater, 30
Balmoral Castle, 5, 28, 32, 38, 39,

86, 102; privacy at, 1, 10; staff
    and officials of, 46, 67; summer
    holiday at, 100, 145, 154–157
Barnes, Barbara, 26, 32, 35
Barnwell Manor, 2, 52
Barratt, John, 12–13, 131–133,
    159
Barry, Stephen, 57–59, 60
Beatrice, Princess, 88, 106,
    111–112; nurseries for, 28, 45;
    parents' holidays and, 23, 34;
    toys for, 35, 39, 40
Beaufort, Duchess of, 96
Beckwith-Smith, Anne, 97
Berneray, Island of, 112–113
Birkhall, 92–93, 107, 113
Blauer, Renate, 81
'Bobo' *see* Macdonald, Margaret
Branson, Richard, 97, 98
Britannia, Royal Yacht, 4, 82, 104,
    115, 120; cost of, 91; Prince
    and Princess of Wales' honey-
    moon aboard, 147, 150,
    151–152, 153; staff and of-
    ficials aboard, 51, 64, 66,

Britannia, Royal Yacht—contd
151–153; Western Isles cruise
aboard, 64, 145, 146–154
Broadlands, 12–13, 84–85, 100–101,
159
Bronnington, H.M.S., 12, 76
Brown, Harold, 54, 55
Bruton Street, 61
Buckingham Palace, 5, 14–15, 16,
71; cost of, 88, 94–95; nursery
at, 31–32, 36, 45, 56; staff and
officials of, 41–59, 77–78,
80–81, 103, 147; wardrobe
store at, 136, 141
Bunn, Nanny, 56
Bush, George, 123
Butler, R.A., 21

Caernarvon, Lord, 87
Callaghan, James, 73
Campbell, Nina, 117
Carrington, Lord, 129
Carter, Jimmy, 121, 130
Cartland, Barbara, 101
Castlewood House, 88, 117
Charles, Prince see Wales, Prince
of
Cheam School, 26, 27
Checketts, Squadron Leader David,
56, 58, 59
Churchill, Winston, 25, 136
Clarence House, 37, 46, 53, 92, 100,
107, 115
Clarke, Felicity, 138
Colebrooke, Miss (Queen's House-
keeper), 46
Cornwall, Duchy of, 49, 89, 112
Cox, Marian, 109
Crawford, Marion ('Crawfie'), 25
Creassey, Lieutenant-Colonel Phi-
lip, 106
Crosby, Bing, 54
Cross, Sergeant Peter, 14

Dalhousie, Lord, 46
Dalton, Richard, 144
de le Bigne, Mme Andrée, 94
Dean, John, 62
Diana, Princess see Wales, Princess
of
Dickman, Cyril, 43
Dunne, Philip, 4, 5, 116, 137

Edelstein, Victor, 144
Edinburgh, Duke of:
(1) royal role and duties, 10, 62,
68, 134, 146; and foreign tours,
119, 124–125; and staff and
officials, 41, 43, 46, 77–78,
98–99;
(2) family and married life, 7,
9–11, 14–15, 19; and children,
26, 27, 36; German relations of,
17, 148; marriage of, 8, 10, 94,
100–101, 134, 159; and nannies
and maids, 56, 57, 60–61;
(3) character and personality, 7,
10, 11, 14, 16, 52, 82; interests
of, 109–110, 127, 145,
146–147, 149; and lead-free
petrol, 129; and money matters, 86–87, 90, 94–95
Edward VII, King, 91
Edward VIII, King, 54, 86–87, 113;
abdication of, 25, 158
Edward, Prince: childhood of,
25–26, 27–28, 30, 35–36, 56,
103, 150; personality of, 77,
115–116; relationship with
father of, 7, 15; visit to Moscow by, 131
Elizabeth, Queen, the Queen
Mother:
(1) royal role and duties, 69, 70–
71, 72, 158; foreign tours of,
121, 126; staff and officials of,
43, 53, 65, 77–78, 114;

(2) family and married life, 8, 10–11, 17, 27; daughters' upbringing by, 9, 24–25, 61, 158; and grandchildren, 35, 112, 114; marriage of, 70, 107;

(3) character and personality, 11, 77, 82, 83–84, 96; clothes and appearance of, 138, 139–140; holidays of, 153–154, 156–157; interests of, 113–115; love of animals, 87, 107, 108; and money matters, 91, 92–93, 100

Elizabeth II, Queen:

(1) role as monarch, 2, 7–8, 111–112, 158–161; accession and Coronation of, 62–63, 159, 160; foreign tours by, 45, 50–51, 66, 91, 119–120, 122, 125, 133; hard work of, 11, 69, 70, 71–74; politics and, 71, 73–74, 136, 160; Silver Jubilee of, 47; staff and officials of, 41–56 passim, 77–78, 79–81, 88, 114;

(2) family and married life, 1–2, 4–5, 7–11 passim, 18–19, 23, 96, 100, 143; children's upbringing by, 25–26, 36, 56, 110; marriage of, 8, 10, 94, 100–101, 134, 159; wedding dress of, 136;

(3) character and personality, 2–4, 7, 11, 12, 16, 20, 21, 134; childhood of, 24–25, 28, 29, 31, 33, 35, 39–40, 73, 108, 158; clothes and appearance of, 3–4, 134–136, 137, 138, 139, 144, 149; and dogs, 3, 38, 48, 102–105, 106; health of, 37, 120; holidays of, 100, 146–157; and horses, 87, 107–108; and money, 86, 87, 90–91, 94;

nicknames of, 45, 77; relaxation and hobbies of, 110, 113, 140, 155; sense of humour of, 71–72, 77, 79–81, 82

Emanuel, David and Elizabeth, 99–100, 136–137, 138, 144

Eton School, 27

Fabiola, Queen, 156

Fagan, Michael, 16

Faisal, King, 97

Fenwick, Mr and Mrs, 103–104

Ferguson, Jane, 31, 37

Ferguson, Major Ronald, 19, 22, 37, 88, 106

Ferguson, Sarah see York, Duchess of

Fermoy, Lady, 83, 116

Fisher, Alan, 54–55

Ford, Gerald, 130

Forwood, Sir Dudley, 70–71

Francis, Dick, 73

Fraser, Domenica, 5

Fraser, Jason, 6

Funafuti, 58

Gatcombe Park, 21, 52, 56, 106

George V, King, 37, 44, 75, 105, 121, 141, 142–143

George VI, King, 37, 43–44, 45, 107, 121, 158; clothes and insignia of, 136, 143; death and funeral of, 16, 62, 70; as husband and father, 9, 10, 24–25, 61, 70, 158

Gibraltar, 39

Gilbert and Ellice Islands, 58

Gilliatt, Sir Martin, 115

Glenconner, Lord, 98

Gloucester, Duchess of, 2, 90–91, 100

Gloucester, Duke of, 2, 90–91; father of, 47, 52, 100

Gorbachev, Mikhail, 131
Gordonstoun School, 17, 26–27
Guards Polo Club, 19

Hall, Ron, 1
Hamilton, Willie, 74
Hammer, Armand, 127
Harry, Prince, 30, 32, 35, 69, 150,
    157; education of, 26, 27, 29;
    health of, 14, 37; pets and toys
    of, 38, 40, 109
Hartnell, Norman, 63, 64, 136, 140
Hastings-Bass, Willie, 87
Heath, Edward, 66
Heggarty, Linda, 111–112
Herne, Major Dick, 87
Highgrove House, 21, 38, 50, 89,
    99, 106, 145
Hill House School, 26, 27
Hillingdon House, 78, 83–84
Hirohito, Emperor, 146
Hoath, Peggy, 64
Hodge, Vicki, 19
Holyroodhouse, Palace of, 46, 71
Hunt, Ward, 18

Jenkins, Roy, 125–126
Juan Carlos, King, 154, 157

Kaye, Danny, 116
Kensington Palace, 27, 36, 55, 95,
    106, 142
Kent, Duchess of, 2, 6, 40, 50,
    90–91; children of, 28; clothes
    of, 137, 138, 144
Kent, Duke of, 2, 40, 50, 90–91
Kent, Prince Michael of, 2, 18–19,
    98, 100, 110
Kent, Princess Michael of: children
    of, 56–57; clothes of, 137, 139,
    143–144; early life of, 18; holi-
    days of, 98, 122; interests of,
    102, 110; and money, 89, 95,

100; public opinion of, 2, 18,
    22, 23, 89; and royal family, 2,
    18–19, 57; staff and officials of,
    50, 51, 55, 56–57
Kenyatta, Jomo, 130
Kerr, Sir John, 84
Kidd, Johnny, 19
Kissinger, Henry, 130
Klosters, 112
Knight, Clara, 24–25, 61
Krushchev, Nikita, 38

Lancaster, Duchy of, 90
Levin, Bernard, 22
Lightbody, Helen, 26, 31–32, 33, 39
Lindsay, Major Hugh, 112
Linley, Viscount, 27–28, 57, 58
Lloyd Webber, Andrew, 116
Lockerbie, 22, 146
Loyd, Alexandra, 53
Loyd, Julian, 53
Lyons, Joe (caterers), 44

McAdam, Denise, 144
McClean, John, 57–59, 75
Macdonald, Margaret ('Bobo'), 25,
    35, 57, 60–67, 103, 135, 137,
    143, 159
Macdonald, Ruby, 25, 35, 65
Mallorca, 154, 157
Marcos, Imelda, 99
Margaret, Princess, 6, 37; child-
    hood of, 10, 24–25, 29, 31, 33,
    35, 39–40, 73, 108, 158; chil-
    dren of, 27–28, 57, 78; clothes
    of, 138, 139; gifts to, 97, 98;
    holidays of, 93, 98, 148; in-
    terests of, 105, 115–116, 153;
    royal duties of, 54, 68, 93, 158;
    and royal family, 9, 10, 18, 75,
    114; staff and officials of, 49,
    54, 57, 65
Martin, Charles, 63, 144

Mary, Queen, 16, 28, 47, 95–96, 121, 136, 140
Menzies, Kate, 5–6
Mey, Castle of, 153–154
Miller, Sir John, 75
Mitterrand, François, 139
Mountbatten of Burma, Earl, 142, 159; assassination of, 11, 16; and money, 100–101; and Prince of Wales, 11–12, 16, 84–85, 142; visits Russia, 131–133
Myers, Norman, 30

Nether Lypiatt, 2, 52
Nettlebed, 2
Newbold, Graham, 106
Newton, Eleanor, 32
Nixon, Richard, 121, 130

Officer, Paul, 57–58, 59, 75
Ogilvy, Angus, 6, 57
Ogilvy, James, 28
Ogilvy, Marina, 28

Parker, Eileen, 9, 33, 65
Parker, Julie, 33
Parker, Michael, 9, 33, 65
Parker Bowles, Camilla, 5
Parliament, State Opening of, 42
Pearce, Joe, 46, 98–99
Peebles, Miss (governess), 26, 29
Philip, Prince see Edinburgh, Duke of
Phillips, Captain Mark, 6–7, 21, 83, 93
Phillips, Peter, 17, 21, 35, 56
Phillips, Zara, 21, 56
Prentice, May, 64
Prince's Jubilee Trust, 90
Princess Royal: childhood of, 25–26, 29–30, 35, 36, 38, 39–40, 109; clothes and appearance of, 139, 144, 149; kidnap attempt on, 128; love of animals, 21, 39, 106, 109, 110; marriage and children of, 6–7, 8, 14, 21, 56, 83, 93; personality of, 13, 14, 20, 21, 54, 91, 93; royal duties of, 20, 21, 22–23, 68, 158; and royal family, 14, 17, 20–22, 69; staff and officials of, 45–46, 52, 54, 56
Private Eye (magazine), 77

Queen see Elizabeth II
Queen Mother see Elizabeth, Queen, the Queen Mother

Rattle, Nanny, 56
Rayne, Edward, 138–139
Reagan, Ronald and Nancy, 7–8, 39, 41–42, 120, 122
Risu, Ritva, 31
Royal Lodge, Windsor, 92, 115
Royal Mews, 42, 128
Royal Navy, 11–12, 23, 75, 76, 88, 147
Royal train, 102, 104, 128
Royal yacht see Britannia
Roberts, Hardy, 44

Sadat, Anwar, 129–130
Sailsbury, Lady, 106
St. James's Palace, 55, 107
St. Laurent, Yves, 89
Salem School, 17
Sandhurst, 81
Sandringham, 1, 2, 64, 69, 86–87, 104, 107–108, 155; car museum at, 129; kennels at, 38, 48, 87; modernization of, 64, 82–83; nursery at, 28; staff and officials of, 46, 49, 53–54, 67
Savary, Peter de, 98
Save the Children Fund, 22–23, 68

Sellers, Peter, 116
Shah of Persia, 50
Shanley, Kevin, 15, 144
Sharp, Dave, 35
Siveright, Pammy, 110
Smallpiece, Sir Basil, 94
Snowdon, Lord, 57, 138
Soames, Nicholas, 58, 123
Somerville, Philip, 137
Spencer, Earl and Countess of, 4, 17–18, 37, 55
Spencer, Lady Diana *see* Wales, Princess of
Spencer, Lady Sarah, 31
Sprecher, Bruno, 112
Stephenson, Pamela, 81
Stronach, Mr and Mrs Ken, 99
Sumner, Nanny, 57
Sunninghill, 21, 31, 117

Thatcher, Margaret, 26, 138
Thomas, Ian, 134, 135
Townsend, Peter, 9, 18
Treetops (Kenya), 62
Trestrail, Commander Michael, 16
Trooping the Colour, 47, 110
Trowbridge, Tom, 18
Trudeau, Pierre, 126
Trump, Donald, 124
Tryon, Lady, 5, 157

United States, 120–5 *passim*
United World Colleges, 122

Vacani, Betty, 33
Victoria, Queen, 71, 94, 95, 96, 143

Wales, Prince of:
  (1) royal role and duties, 69–70, 72, 73, 146, 160–161; engagements, 122, 123; foreign tours by, 74–75, 119, 121–126 *passim*, 129–131; gifts to, 97, 98, 99;
  (2) marriage and family life, 4–5, 31, 56, 87–88, 124; children, 26, 27, 29, 35, 56, 69, 97; honeymoon, 127, 147, 150, 151–152, 153; in-laws, 17–18; pre-marriage friends, 5, 59, 155; staff and officials, 43, 45, 48, 50, 52–59 *passim*, 75, 89, 114; *see also* Harry, Prince; William, Prince;
  (3) character and personality, 7, 13–14, 16–17; cars of, 91–92, 129; childhood of, 25–40 *passim*, 62, 109, 112–113, 114; clothes of, 140–143, 149; holidays of, 5, 58–59, 154, 157; interests and hobbies of, 105–106, 108, 109, 111, 127, 145, 150; and money, 87–88, 89–90, 91, 94; and Earl Mountbatten, 11–12, 16, 84–85, 142; naval career of, 11–12, 75, 76, 147; and royal family, 7, 8, 11, 19–20; sense of humour of, 76–77, 153
Wales, Princess of: and animals, 21, 102, 105–106, 108–109; character of, 3, 15, 31, 123; childhood of, 27, 29, 31, 37, 97, 108; clothes of, 124, 125, 136–138, 139, 143, 144, 149; on foreign tours, 121–123, 124, 125, 129; on holidays, 149, 154, 155, 157; interests and hobbies of, 33, 111, 116–117; marriage *see under* Wales, Prince of; and money, 87–88, 89–90, 92, 124; presents to, 97, 99–100; royal duties and role of, 1, 15, 68–69, 116; and royal family, 2, 15, 19, 20–21, 69
Walker, Catherine, 137–138, 144
Wallace, Ruth, 56–57

Walwyn, Fulke, 87
Wardley, Alison, 88
Waterhouse, Major David, 6
Westminster Abbey, 62–63
Wetherby School, 26, 29
Wharf, Ken, 6
Wilkin, Sir Michael, 7
William, Prince, 69, 150, 157; education of, 26, 27, 29; personality of, 28–29, 30, 32, 35; pets and toys of, 38, 39, 109
Williams, Ian, 35
Wilson, Harold, 73–74
Windsor, Duke of *see* Edward VIII
Windsor Castle, 2, 65, 73, 103, 107–108, 145; Gorbachev's visit, 131; nursery at, 28; Reagan's visit, 7–8, 41–42; staff and officials of, 41–42, 45, 46, 49; in wartime, 25, 61
Winskill, Archie, 114

York, Duchess of: childhood of, 31, 37, 40; clothes and appearance of, 138, 144; interests and hobbies of, 3, 106, 117–118, 150, 154, 155; marriage of, 21, 22, 23, 34, 88–89, 117–118; and money, 88–89, 90; personality of, 15, 22, 81, 116; public opinion of, 6, 22–23, 34, 89; royal duties of, 68, 69, 118; and royal family, 2, 15, 21–22, 23; wedding of, 134, 136
York, Duke of: childhood of, 25–30 *passim*, 35–36, 39, 56, 150; interests and hobbies of, 110, 117, 150, 155; marriage of, 21, 22, 23, 34, 88–89, 117–118; naval career of, 23, 88, 147; personality of, 14–15, 22, 23; royal duties of, 19, 22, 69; and royal family, 14, 19–20, 22